DARIO FO

Dario Fo, an Italian actor-author, can claim to be one of the most frequently performed playwrights in the world. Born on Lake Maggiore in northern Italy on 24 March 1926, he made his debut in theatre in 1952, and was writing, performing and painting until fifteen days before his death, on 13 October 2016. His work went through various phases, always in company with his wife, the actress Franca Rame. His stage career began with political cabaret, moved on to one-act farces, and then to satirical comedies in his so-called 'bourgeois phase' in the early 1960s, when he became a celebrated figure on TV and in Italy's major theatres. In 1968, he broke with conventional theatre to set up a cooperative dedicated to producing politically committed work in what were then known as 'alternative venues'. His best-known plays, including *Mistero Buffo* (1969), *Accidental Death of an Anarchist* (1970) and *Trumpets and Raspberries* (1981), date from this period. He was awarded the Nobel Prize for Literature in 1997 and, in the official citation, the Swedish Royal Academy stated that he had 'emulated the jesters of the Middle Ages in scourging authority and upholding the dignity of the downtrodden'.

FRANCA RAME

Franca Rame was born in Parabiago, north-west Milan, on 18 July 1929. Daughter of Domenico Rame and Emilia Fo, both wandering minstrels, she was born into a family with strong theatrical traditions: Famiglia Rame. She made her theatrical debut as a child and in 1950 left her home and family to begin her career in theatre, film and television. In 1958, alongside her husband, Dario Fo, she founded the Theatre Company of Dario Fo Franca Rame (Compagnia Teatrale Dario Fo Franca Rame). She wrote comedies on the female condition such as *The Rape* (1975), *Open Couple* (1983), *Let's Talk About Women* (1991), *Settimo Steals a Little Less* (1992), *Sex? Don't Mind If I Do*

(1996) and *Mother Peace: Let Mothers Decide About War* (2005). She also collaborated on all of Dario Fo's works. In the 1970s she founded Red Aid and in 1988 the Nobel Committee for the Disabled. Her awards include the Obie Prize (New York, 1987), Leon Felipe for Human Rights (Spain, 1998), Vittorini Prize (Siracusa, 1998), an Honorary Fellowship (Wolverhampton University, 1998), a Lifetime Achievement Award (Harvard University and Columbia University, 2001), an Honorary Degree (Middlebury College, Vermont, 2008), Vittorio De Sica Award (Quirinale, 2011), Research Doctorate in Music and Entertainment (Sapienza University of Rome, 2014). From 2006–8 she was a Senator of the Republic. She died in Milan on 29 May 2013.

TOM BASDEN

Tom Basden's other plays include *The Crocodile* (Manchester International Festival); *Holes* (Edinburgh Festival Fringe/Arcola Theatre, London); *There is a War* (as part of the Double Feature season in the Paintframe at the National Theatre); *Joseph K* (Gate Theatre, London); and *Party* (Fringe First Winner; Edinburgh Festival Fringe/Sydney International Festival/Arts Theatre, London). For television, he co-created *Plebs* for ITV2; the sketch show *Cowards* for BBC Four; *Gap Year* for E4; and wrote and starred in *Here We Go* for BBC One. Tom has also written episodes of *Peep Show*, *Fresh Meat* and *The Wrong Mans*. For Radio 4 he has made two series of *Cowards*, and three series and a Christmas special of his sitcom *Party*.

Dario Fo and Franca Rame

ACCIDENTAL DEATH OF AN ANARCHIST

adapted by
Tom Basden

NICK HERN BOOKS

London

www.nickhernbooks.co.uk

A Nick Hern Book

This adaptation of *Accidental Death of an Anarchist* first published as a paperback original in Great Britain in 2022 by Nick Hern Books Limited, The Glasshouse, 49a Goldhawk Road, London W12 8QP

This edition with revisions and a new cover published in 2023

Morte accidentale di un anarchico copyright © 1970 Dario Fo and Franca Rame; copyright © 2018 Ugo Guanda Editore S.r.l., Milano
This adaptation of *Accidental Death of an Anarchist* copyright © 2023 Tom Basden

Tom Basden has asserted his right to be identified as the author of this adaptation

Cover image: Daniel Rigby as the Maniac, photography by Jennifer McCord, design by Greg Bunbury

Designed and typeset by Nick Hern Books, London
Printed in the UK by Mimeo Ltd, Huntingdon, Cambridgeshire PE29 6XX

ISBN   978 1 83904 254 6

www.nickhernbooks.co.uk/environmental-policy

This adaptation of *Accidental Death of an Anarchist* was
commissioned by Holly Reiss and developed for the West End
by Matthew Byam Shaw and Jack Lea for Playful Productions.

It received its West End premiere at the Theatre Royal
Haymarket, London, on 12 June 2023, presented by Matthew
Byam Shaw, Nia Janis and Nick Salmon for Playful
Productions, Holly Reiss, Len Blavatnik and Danny Cohen for
Access Entertainment, Karl Sydow for Dance with Mr D,
Playing Field, Eric Kuhn and Tulchin/Bartner. The cast and
creative team was as follows:

THE MANIAC	Daniel Rigby
SUPERINTENDENT CURRY	Tony Gardner
DETECTIVE DAN DAISY	Tom Andrews
INSPECTOR BURTON	Mark Hadfield
PC JOSEPH	Ro Kumar
PC JACKSON/FI PHELAN	Ruby Thomas

Director	Daniel Raggett
Set and Costume Designer	Anna Reid
Lighting Designer	Jai Morjaria
Sound Designer & Composer	Annie May Fletcher
Video Designer	Matt Powell
Additional Musical Arrangements & Supervision	Nick Barstow
Fight Director	Kenan Ali
Casting Director	Lotte Hines CDG
Production Manager	Juli Fraire
Associate Director	George Jibson
Associate Producer	Jack Lea
Costume Supervisor	Binnie Bowerman
Company Stage Manager	Paul Ferris
Deputy Stage Manager	Ray Young
Assistant Stage Manager	Bella Kelaidi

Prior to this, the adaptation was first performed at the Playhouse, Sheffield Theatres, on 23 September 2022, with the following cast:

THE MANIAC	Daniel Rigby
SUPERINTENDENT CURRY	Tony Gardner
DETECTIVE DAN DAISY	Jordan Metcalfe
INSPECTOR BURTON	Howard Ward
PC JOSEPH	Shane David-Joseph
PC JACKSON/FI PHELAN	Ruby Thomas

The production transferred to the Lyric Hammersmith Theatre, London, on 13 March 2023, with the same cast, and presented by arrangement with Jamie Hendry.

Characters

MANIAC – *an unnamed, compulsive performer, the only
    character able to see the audience*
BURTON – *Inspector Burton, from the third floor*
SUPERINTENDENT – *Superintendent Curry, the station chief*
DAISY – *Detective Daisy, a plain-clothes detective*
JACKSON – *PC Jackson, from the third floor*
JOSEPH – *Agent Joseph, the superintendant's aide*
PHELAN – *Fi Phelan, a journalist*
RANDALL – *Judge Randall, also played by the Maniac*

*This text went to press before the end of rehearsals and so may
differ slightly from the play as performed.*

ACT ONE

Scene One

A very normal-looking room in a police station. It has a wooden desk and chair and a small filing cabinet.

There is a large Metropolitan Police crest on the wall. And a number '3'. And a clock, stopped at 5:15. On the desk is a telephone. There are two doors and, to one side, a large window. A view of the city can be seen from it.

The MANIAC *enters, clutching a large Liberty bag. He stands, putting the bag down, and walks around the stage, smiling and waving to the audience, taking in the ambience, smelling the space. Music plays.*

INSPECTOR BURTON *enters, carrying a folder and laptop, and hangs up his overcoat on the back of his chair and then sits.* CONSTABLE JACKSON *enters after and stands by the door.* BURTON *looks around, confused.*

BURTON. Turn it off!

The MANIAC *takes out a small tape player from his bag and turns it off. He stands and begins to stretch. First the arms. Then the calves. He squats.* BURTON *puts his laptop on the desk. And then looks up at the* MANIAC, *angrily.*

Sit down!

The MANIAC *does so. He stretches his neck as* BURTON *opens the folder. The* MANIAC *clears his throat.* BURTON *looks at him. And then resumes reading.*

MANIAC. *Mi mi mi mi mi…*

BURTON. And shut up.

The MANIAC *does so.*

Flight attendant, naval engineer, minor royal… quite the repertoire you've got, isn't it?

MANIAC. Thank you very much.

BURTON. Heart surgeon?! Bloody hell!

MANIAC. A theatre's a theatre, Inspector, be it West End or operating. I'm not fussy, I'll work anywhere.

BURTON. So I see. Translator for the Russian Embassy. You speak Russian then, do you?

MANIAC. Ha! No, not a word.

BURTON. So how did you manage that then?

MANIAC. Oh don't be obtuse, man. A good translation does not reproduce the source material word for word, it captures the essence, not the detail. And in the case of the Russian Embassy, the essence of every press release or communiqué is always 'The accusation is outrageous and anyway you did it first...'

BURTON. All told, we're talking... five, six –

MANIAC. Twelve.

  BURTON *flicks through the file as the* MANIAC *creeps round to read over his shoulder.*

BURTON. Eight, nine –

MANIAC. It is twelve –

BURTON. Twelve arrests for impersonation –

MANIAC. But not a single charge. As you can see, my record is unsullied.

BURTON. Yeah, not for long. I don't know how you've got away with it so far, but you're getting sullied today, I promise you.

  The MANIAC *puts his arm around him coyly.*

MANIAC. Please be gentle, Inspector, it's my first time.

  BURTON *pushes him away.*

BURTON. So what is it now then? Therapist.

MANIAC. Psychiatrist, actually.

BURTON *finds a business card.*

BURTON. 'Senior Professor of Psychiatrics, Wadham College Oxford.' Ha! Well that's a crime right off. Inventing qualifications.

MANIAC. Of course it is. Fabricating doctorates, degrees, identities would be a criminal offence if I were sane. But I'm sadly not.

BURTON. You're what?

MANIAC. I'm not.

BURTON. You're not what?

MANIAC. Sane. I'm mad.

BURTON. Is that right?

MANIAC. It is. Certifiable. Literally, look.

He takes a framed certificate out of his bag and passes it to BURTON.

None of it is my fault. I have a serious mental illness.

BURTON. Which is what exactly?

MANIAC. The desire to act. '*Istrionomania*' to give it its technical name.

BURTON *writes this down.*

BURTON. Istro... what?

MANIAC. Istrionomania. From the Italian *istrione*, meaning classical actor, with the hint of the ham. *Istrione al proscuitto crudo* if you will. The condition of compulsively needing to perform, anywhere, anyone, any time. Hence my pathological fear of the dark.

BURTON. What... Why?

MANIAC. Well because blackouts are very death to the actor. I am always on, Inspector. So it's essential that the lights are as well.

BURTON. Jesus... you're kidding me. You're like this all the time?

MANIAC. I'm afraid so, yes. All the world's a stage for me.
I think of daily life as a kind of *théâtre vérité* in which the
rest of the cast are made up of non-actors who are unaware
that a show is taking place. Which is lucky because
I couldn't afford to pay them.

BURTON. Looks like you could afford it now though, doesn't
it? You could afford to *build* a bloody theatre with the money
you've been making as a so-called therapist.

MANIAC. Psychiatrist! How dare you!

BURTON. What's the difference?

MANIAC. Psychiatrists can charge far more.

BURTON. Right, yeah… Five grand per session.

JACKSON. Fucking hell.

MANIAC. I know. Very cheap really when you consider my
training…

BURTON. What training's that? Drama school?

MANIAC. Almost. Mental hospital. Twenty years at sixteen
different institutions, among the thousands of patients like
myself. I've studied them up close, not just nine-to-five like
your average workaday shrink, but twenty-four-seven. I've
eaten with them, showered with them, slept with them.
Among them, I've not – I've very rarely slept with them.
QED I am prodigiously good at knowing what makes people
tick. Or tock. Or quack, depending on the condition.

BURTON. I should hope so. Thirty-five grand you've charged
people so far.

MANIAC. But, my dear Inspector, I had to charge that much.
For my patients' sake.

BURTON. Oh it was for their sake, was it?

MANIAC. Of course. The more you cost, the more you're
worth. The more people think you know what you're doing.
Was it not Freud who said, 'To truly cure the mentally ill,
add some zeros to your bill.' It has enormous health benefits,
I assure you, particularly for the doctor.

BURTON. But you're not a doctor, are you? And you're certainly not... (*Reads*.) 'Antony Bile: MA, Senior Professor of Psychiatrics, Wadham College Oxford.'

MANIAC. I never said I was.

BURTON. Of course you did. You've got a bloody business card.

MANIAC. Business card? Who said it was a business card?

BURTON. Well what is it then?

MANIAC. It's very clearly a script.

BURTON. A what? A script?

MANIAC. The pages are small, I grant you, but the formatting is unmistakable. Look at the punctuation. (*Reads*.) Antony Bile, colon, indicating that what follows is of course my line.

BURTON. Okay, go on then, so you say... M-A.

MANIAC. I say 'Ma'. Well I shout it. It's capitalised because I'm shouting you see. 'MA!' I'm calling my mother. And then I turn to the members of our group, hence the comma, to signify a shift of perspective and say 'Senior Professor of Psychiatrics' to get his attention and then another comma as I turn to the spire that looms up ahead, 'Wadham College Oxford.' We're approaching by bus, you see. This is all perfectly clear in context.

BURTON. You really expect me to believe this is from a play?

MANIAC. Of course, I'll perform if for you.

The MANIAC *acts sitting on a bus. And seeing something.*

'MA, Senior Professor of Psychiatrics, Wadham College Oxford!'

BURTON. That's fucking rubbish.

MANIAC (*offended*). Well you clearly haven't seen much theatre. I can give you a crash course if you like. We'll start with the Greeks and work our way west.

BURTON. Yeah, yeah, I know what this is. I'm not an idiot, you know?

MANIAC. Oh, are you not? Good for you.

BURTON. I've seen this before.

MANIAC. Quite possibly. It was first staged in 1970.

BURTON. You're acting alright. You're acting like a loony so I let you go. I bet, underneath it all, you're saner than I am.

The MANIAC *takes a stethoscope from his bag and launches himself at* BURTON *over the desk.*

MANIAC. Well I wouldn't know. Let's have a look at you and find out. Pop your trousers on the desk for me –

BURTON *pushes him away.*

BURTON. And it won't work. Not with me. I'm going to finish this statement and see that this gets taken seriously.

MANIAC. Fantastic. Let me help! I can type sixty words a minute, as long as the words are 'A' or 'I'.

The MANIAC *tries to start typing on the laptop keyboard.*

BURTON. Sit down or I'll cuff you –

MANIAC. Ah bless. No, I'm sorry, you won't. Section 136 of the Mental Health Act. Without an assessment from an AHCP (appropriate healthcare practitioner) and the presence of an AMHP (approved mental health professional) I'm afraid you can do AFFOFEOFA – about four-fifths of five-eighths of fuck-all.

BURTON. So you're a legal expert as well, are you?

MANIAC. I am actually. I was fortunate enough to share a cell with a schizophrenic attorney general. He taught me every law out there – criminal, civil, medical, military, sharia, Newtonian, Murphy's, Sod's.

BURTON *(checks the file)*. Huh. And yet you've never impersonated a lawyer?

MANIAC. Oh no, I'd hate that. Having to bother with tedious things like juries and facts. No, no, I want to decide the truth for myself and assemble the evidence accordingly – like the brave men and women of the Metropolitan Police.

BURTON *stands.*

BURTON. Watch it!

MANIAC. Officer, I'm paying you a compliment. I'm saying, yours is a far more artistic career than that of the lawyer. It requires genuine invention and panache. I'm not being sarky, I swear.

BURTON. Okay, well, I'll be the judge of that –

MANIAC. Oh, now you're talking! How I would love to play a judge. *Ai me!* The power, the dignity! You hit sixty, sixty-five, just as you should be tossed on the scrapheap, you're suddenly in your prime.

The MANIAC *sits in* BURTON'*s chair.*

Just as factory workers are getting RSI, brickies are getting asbestosis, cabbies can't remember where the A2 is, judges are just getting going. Seventy, eighty, ninety, deaf, senile, incontinent, never you mind, you crack on, old boy. As long as you can send people down we'll keep promoting you. They only bang that hammer thingy to keep themselves awake… Order!

The MANIAC *bangs his fist on the desk.*

Order! Someone order me a gin fizz!

BURTON. Stop banging, you bloody loony!

BURTON *goes to restrain him. The* MANIAC *spins round.*

MANIAC. Hands off me or I'll bite!

BURTON. And get out of my chair!

MANIAC. Make me.

BURTON (*to* JACKSON). Make him!

JACKSON. He'll bite me.

BURTON. Of course he won't.

MANIAC. I might. I might bite. I am a bit of a biter. I blame the rabies.

BURTON *walks over to the door and opens it.*

BURTON. Alright, fuck this, you win, get out. I don't need this, you can go.

MANIAC. Oh no please, Inspector, please don't kick me out! Just as we're becoming friends. I beg you...

BURTON. Out! Go on! I've got enough to deal with as it is.

The MANIAC *springs up and makes for the desk.*

MANIAC. Then let me help! I can be the Watson to your Holmes. I can make people talk! I know how to waterboard! Or wineboard! Or cheeseboard! I know how to punch people without leaving a bruise! I'll be a credit to the force. At least give me an application form!

BURTON. Piss off!

BURTON *heads for the* MANIAC. *He jinks away, around the desk to the window.*

MANIAC. No, please, it's dangerous out there. The streets are heaving with electric scooters and bad tattoos and children wielding breadknives!

I can't go back, I can't, I... I'll throw myself out the window!

BURTON *freezes.*

JACKSON. Oh my God, not another one.

MANIAC. What? What's this? Another what?

BURTON. Nothing. She didn't say anything.

MANIAC. But of course. This is where the poor sod flung himself out of the window! This very police station.

BURTON. It is, yeah –

MANIAC. Well now! This is a famous building! You should have a blue plaque. This window frame should be a UNESCO World Heritage Site.

BURTON. It wasn't this window, it was the one on the floor above. And don't get any ideas, you're not jumping. Shut it, Constable.

JACKSON. I didn't say anything.

BURTON. The window.

JACKSON. Yes. Sorry.

She does so.

BURTON. Now… get out!

He grabs the MANIAC *by the arm and flings him outside.*

MANIAC. Don't touch me, I've got worms! And intimacy issues.

BURTON *shuts the door after him. Beat.*

BURTON. Jesus Christ. I need a nap.

JACKSON. I'm afraid you've got another diversity and inclusion training session, sir.

BURTON. Oh for… What is it this time?

JACKSON. Unconscious bias, sir.

BURTON. Ugh. I don't even know what unconscious bias is and I bloody hate it…

JACKSON. Yes, I think that's sort of how it works.

BURTON *wheezes to his feet. And leaves from the other door, leaving it open.* JACKSON *follows him, leaving the room empty.*

Beat. Then light knocking at the closed door.

MANIAC. Hello? Inspector Burton? I don't mean to be a pain but, in my rather hasty exit, I appear to have left all of my props. Inspector? Don't sulk. I'm sorry too. I hate it when we fight like this. Inspector?

The MANIAC *opens the door. And peers inside.*

Mm. No one at the inn. I'll just take the liberty of taking my Liberty bag.

He picks it up. And starts taking papers from the desk.

And my medical records. And my tiny play. And the rest, as they say, is silence. Or, well actually, let's have a quick squizz at these charge sheets… while I'm here…

The MANIAC *picks up some other folders on the desk.*
While he does so he walks over to the window and opens it.

Ooh! 'Glueing yourself to the A4.' Pfff. That's nothing!
Probably just crashed into a Copydex lorry. You're free,
sonny Jim!

Flings the file out of the window. Looks at the next one.

What about you? 'Violent protest on Clapham Common.'
What would that be? Headbutting a riot police baton while
sitting on the floor? Good for you, girl. Case dismissed. *Fly,*
my pretties, fly!

He flings lots of files of the window.

The phone rings. The MANIAC *looks at it. And winces.*

Ooh... I shouldn't. But I want to. But I shouldn't. But I will.

He walks over to the phone. Stops. And looks at the
audience.

If I don't answer it of course we could all just go to the bar.
It's very tempting I must say.

(*Weighing it up.*) Ah, what the hell.

He picks up the phone. And immediately assumes another
voice.

'Ello 'ello 'ello, Inspector Burton's office. To whom am
I speaking please? From the fourth floor! Then you must be
Detective Window-Straddler himself? I'm star-struck,
I really am. Window-Straddler. Well that's just what Burton
calls you down here. Alright, calm down, I know you didn't.
I know it was an accident, yes, the inquiry said so. Exactly.
Hang on, I'll check.

He covers the phone for a moment.

No, I can't put you through to Bertie. Burton. He says he's
not here. Well I imagine because he doesn't want to talk to
you. No. So just tell me what it is and I'll – My name? Plod.
Plod. Well Sergeant Plod actually, I've been promoted. Okay,
what do you need? The judge's verdict, yup, I can bring that
up. Anything else? Witness statements, sure.

(*Looking around the room*.) Bertie? Where are the files for the guy who got thrown out of the window? Jumped! Sorry, the guy who got jumped out of the window?

He opens the drawer in the filing cabinet.

Here we go. 'The Accidental Death of an Anarchist.' Yes, I've found it! What do you need it for? Reopening the inquiry? Why? They think it ended prematurely? Yes I've heard you've got that problem. Huh? No, nothing. So which judge is it this time? Judge Randall! Indeed I do. He's an absolute ball-breaker. Well you'll be fine then. If you're innocent, I'm sure top brass will support you wholeheartedly...

Laughs.

Huh? No, it's just Bertie's saying that the chief constable's going to throw you under the bus. Ha! He's doing quite an elaborate mime with you being run over by a Routemaster, it's actually very athletic. Oh Bertie, that's hilarious!

Laughs.

Well he's now miming your brains coming out of your ears and... What are you doing now, Bertie? Oh I see, he's reversing!

Laughs.

Yes, he's repeatedly going over your head with the – Oh now, come on, Detective, don't be like that! It's only a joke. Of course it is! Like when us coppers take selfies with murder victims! It's classic bants. Well I think you're massively overreacting, mate. Sure, yeah, I'll tell him. Bertie – the window-flinging detective from upstairs is going to punch you in the face when he next sees you. Yes. Well Bertie's saying bring it on and is miming doing a shit on your corpse Right-o. Bye then.

The MANIAC *hangs up the phone.*

A judge! Oh heavens! Oh finally! This is the role I was born to play! Come with me now, as we go inside the actor's studio. First I need to age up a bit of course...

He takes out an old-man mask.

Alas, poor Rupert Murdoch – I knew him, Horatio. Bit much?

He puts it back. And takes out a bottle of talcum powder from his bag and shakes it onto his hair.

There we are... science!

(*Changing his voice.*) Judge Randall presiding! Ooh, if I can pull this one off I can really put on a show! Now then... glasses! But which ones?

The MANIAC *takes out some glasses and tries them on.*

What do you think? No, nor me... what about...?

He tries on some half-moon glasses.

The half-moons, of course! Perched on the tip of the trunk so I have to look down my nose at everyone...

He removes his jacket, addressing someone in the front row.

How do you feel about the fourth wall?

He flings his jacket at them.

Too late!

Then picks up BURTON*'s overcoat and puts it on.*

Make way for Judge Randall!

He flicks through the file.

Here to inquire into the activities of a seditious anarchist group led by... a male dancer apparently...

BURTON *comes back in with* JACKSON.

BURTON. Oh. Hi, sorry, are you... Can I help you?

MANIAC. No thank you, Inspector. I just popped back to collect my papers.

BURTON. Oh my God, not you again! I thought I told you to piss off!

MANIAC. Calm down, dear, I know it's a stressful job, but don't take it out on me –

BURTON. Get out!

MANIAC. What is wrong with you people today? First there's the psycho detective going around saying he wants to punch you in the face –

BURTON. What? Punch me?

MANIAC. In the face, yes. And then there's you roaring away like Gordon Ramsay after a disappointing risotto –

BURTON. Why are you still here? Go away!

MANIAC. I'm going! Look, I'm clearly exiting stage-left as we speak. So long, farewell, auf wiedersehen, goodnight, ladies, sweet ladies, goodnight, goodnight.

The MANIAC *blows a kiss to the audience and then back to* BURTON – *giving him a big hug.*

I'll miss you most of all, Scarecrow!

BURTON. Get off me!

MANIAC. No tears, Inspector. Be strong for Mummy. We'll meet again. One sunny day. When the hurly-burly's done. When the battle's lost and won, et cetera.

BURTON. Eff off.

MANIAC. Effing off as we speak, sir!

(*Salutes.*) Oh, remember to duck, won't you?

BURTON. What? Duck?

MANIAC. When you see the detective from the fourth floor, duck.

The MANIAC *exits and shuts the door.* BURTON *returns to his desk, sits and exhales. And looks around.*

BURTON. Oh shit! My overcoat…

He reopens the door, but there's no sign of the MANIAC. BURTON *returns to his desk and picks up the phone.*

Get me front desk. It's Burton – listen, there's a maniac on his way out wearing my coat. Uh, beige. Single-breasted, wool. Oh I see. Male. Thirties.

He heads for the other door and opens it.

Average height. Average face. Average everything.

He spots someone approaching and covers the phone.

Oh! Detective, don't suppose you've seen a maniac around who's nicked my coat? He mentioned you as it goes, said you were gonna –

A fist from offstage punches him in the face. He falls against the doorframe, groaning. The MANIAC *opens the other door.*

MANIAC....punch you in the face, yes. I did tell you to duck!

The MANIAC *pushes* BURTON *out of the door and picks up the phone and presses a button.*

Fourth floor please? Pass on a message to Detective Window-Straddler, will you? Tell him I demand an audience at once. I'll be in his office.

The MANIAC *rearranges the '3' on the wall into a '4'.*

Please remain in your seats, ladies and gentlemen, as we make our way to the fourth floor. Pardon me while I employ a little feng shui.

He flings the laptop out of the window.

In the event of turbulence or a sudden loss of pressure please feel free to grab the thigh of the person sitting next to you...

Scene Two

The MANIAC *walks over the window and pulls on a cord which appears to be the blinds but actually makes the view of the city outside go up by one floor.*

MANIAC. Right, that should do it.

The MANIAC *sets his hat at the right angle and sits in the chair, facing the audience.*

Mi mi mi mi…

AGENT JOSEPH *opens the door.* DETECTIVE DAISY *follows him in, massaging his hand.*

DAISY. But who is he? What does he want?

JOSEPH. I don't know, sir, sorry, he just started yelling at me and demanded an audience.

DAISY. A what?

JOSEPH. An audience? With the detective from the fourth floor, yes, sorry.

DAISY spots the MANIAC *in the chair.*

DAISY. Alright, go on then, talk to me.

The MANIAC *swivels round dramatically.*

MANIAC. Good day.

DAISY. Yeah, hi, DI Dan Daisy, what's this all about?

MANIAC. What have you done to your hand?

DAISY. Oh, nothing, look, who are you?

DAISY sits opposite him.

MANIAC. Nothing? Why are you rubbing it like that then? I thought policemen were always massaging the figures, not the fingers. Ha!

DAISY. Yeah. Funny. Who are you?

MANIAC. I once knew a Catholic priest who used to do that. Not to himself though. What is it, a nervous tic? Oh deary me…

DAISY. I said it's nothing –

MANIAC. Classic sign of insecurity, guilt, sexual inadequacy. I can recommend a very good psychiatrist in fact.

The MANIAC *offers* DAISY *a business card.*

DAISY. Don't fucking push it, alright?

MANIAC. Well you're certainly not insecure. Maybe I got you wrong. Maybe there's nothing wrong with your noggin at all, you just punched someone with that hand a few moments ago.

DAISY. Uh-huh. Detective, are you?

MANIAC. No. The Right Honourable Lord Justice Judge Arnold Nathaniel Randall.

DAISY. Judge…

MANIAC. Arnold Nathaniel Randall, yes. My pronouns are 'We' and 'Us'. You'd been tipped off that I was coming, surely? Given the warning to dot the 'I's and do up your flies…?

DAISY. I… No –

MANIAC. Please don't lie, I can't bear lies, they make me gag, you see?

The MANIAC *starts to dry heave.*

DAISY. Yeah, no, I, we did know you were coming, my worship, but didn't realise it would be so soon.

MANIAC. Well it is so soon. I trust my being here doesn't make you nervous –

DAISY. No, no, not at all.

The MANIAC *goes to throw up again.*

Or, maybe a little bit, but only because this 'Death of the Anarchist' case was meant to be over ages ago –

MANIAC. Well the initial inquiry is over, yes, but that wasn't inquisitive enough, so now there's an inquiry into that. It's the British way, of course. Inquiries into inquiries into inquiries for as long as it takes for everyone involved to destroy the evidence and change careers. If God were British, there wouldn't be a Judgement Day, there'd be an eternal fucking inquiry.

He laughs. DAISY *laughs along. The* MANIAC *stops at once.*

It's no laughing matter.

DAISY. No. Quite right, your liege.

MANIAC. M'lud.

DAISY. Y'lud.

MANIAC. Call in the superintendent, will you, Daisy? Let's get this show on the road.

DAISY. Yes of course. You're sure you wouldn't be more comfortable in his office, y'lud? There are beanbags.

MANIAC. No, no, this is where it all happened, is it not? This window is the scene of the crime. This very void is our murder weapon, gravity herself the murderer.

DAISY. Sure, yeah, you could say that.

MANIAC. I know I could. I did.

The MANIAC *sits and takes out various objects from the Liberty bag: documents, pliers, a magnifying glass, a gavel.* DAISY *and* JOSEPH *talk discreetly during this.*

A bit louder please, Detective. Whispering seems a little unfair on the people in the cheap seats.

DAISY. Right, yeah, soz –

(*To* JOSEPH.) Ask the superintendent to come down sharpish if he can.

MANIAC. Or if he can't.

DAISY. Or if he can't, exactly.

JOSEPH. Yes, sir.

JOSEPH *leaves*. DAISY *reaches for the phone*.

DAISY. Hi there. This is Dan Daisy. Hope you're having a great day. Would it be possible to put me through to Burton please? Or Plod? Plod.

MANIAC. We shan't be needing them, Detective –

DAISY. They've the got all the paperwork down there, y'lud –

MANIAC. I have it here. Everything from the initial inquiry… statements, reports, hotel expenses…

DAISY. Okay, sweet.

> DAISY *puts the phone back in its cradle. From off we hear someone approaching*.

SUPERINTENDENT. WHERE'S DAISY?

MANIAC. Aha. Bang on cue.

> *The* MANIAC *sets himself to watch the chaos unfold. The door opens and* SUPERINTENDENT CURRY *storms in, furious, and heads for* DAISY. JOSEPH *follows, holding a mug of tea*.

SUPERINTENDENT. What the hot fuck is all this about getting me to come here as soon as I can or I can't?

DAISY. No, I know, sir, I think that may have been lost in translation –

SUPERINTENDENT. 'Translation' my absolute arsehole, to be honest. You need to get some respect going, mate. You cannot talk to me like that. And you cannot go round punching colleagues in the face. End of.

DAISY. You didn't see the mime Burton was doing, sir –

SUPERINTENDENT. Nor did you, you were on the phone –

DAISY. Well yeah but –

SUPERINTENDENT. Yeah but shut up. And calm down! A bit of professionalism. Please. Is what we need. Here. There are hacks and film crews everywhere trying to dig up dirt on us. There's a bloody journalist on her way over now. Once upon a time, we'd have undercover cops working as informers, now there are undercover informers working as cops. It's absolute hell-in-a-handcart time. No more hitting. Please. You need to pull your finger out your arse and keep your nose clean.

MANIAC. With a different finger I hope.

SUPERINTENDENT. With a different finger, exactly, what?

He suddenly sees the MANIAC.

Who's that? Are you a journalist? What's going on?

MANIAC. No, no, don't panic, Superintendent, I'm not a journalist, I assure you, I'm just enjoying the show.

SUPERINTENDENT. Alright, well…

MANIAC. But I totally agree, your detective here could do with a little anger-management work. I can recommend a terrific psychiatrist actually…

The MANIAC *passes the* SUPERINTENDENT *a business card.*

SUPERINTENDENT. Okay, yeah, we'll bear that in mind, sorry, I don't believe we've met –

MANIAC. Indeed not, Lord Chief Justice Judge Arnold Nathaniel Randall.

SUPERINTENDENT. Oh! Yes. Of course. Wonderful to meet you at last.

MANIAC. I'm delighted to be here.

SUPERINTENDENT. It's my honour, your honour.

They shake hands. The MANIAC *brushes some talc off his arms and shoulders, causing the* SUPERINTENDENT *to splutter.*

MANIAC. Indeed. Please do pardon my dandruff.

SUPERINTENDENT. I didn't even notice it.

DAISY. He's here to conduct another inquiry, sir –

SUPERINTENDENT. Yes. We were expecting you, m'lud.

MANIAC. I know. And I thank you for your frankness.

(*To* DAISY.) You could learn a lot from this man, Daisy. No hidden agenda, no subterfuge, just common-or-garden plain speaking. These are the people that won us the war, you see.

SUPERINTENDENT. Well, yes and no, I'm only fifty-eight –

MANIAC. But you have a maturity beyond your years, Superintendent. The earthy zeal of a colonial hero. A Cecil Rhodes, a Clive of India, winning over the natives through a combination of ball games and starvation.

SUPERINTENDENT. Right, well, thank you. Forgive me for asking but which inquiry are you here about, m'lud? There have been a few recently.

The SUPERINTENDENT *takes the tea from* JOSEPH.

MANIAC. I'll say! Two or three Met officers will face criminal charges every week from now on, they tell me –

SUPERINTENDENT. Oh it's getting silly.

MANIAC. You poor loves. It must be a nightmare just keeping track of all the investigations these days…

SUPERINTENDENT. We're doing our best.

MANIAC. If only that were true.

The MANIAC *laughs. The* SUPERINTENDENT *smiles fawningly.*

This one is concerning a recent death that happened in police custody.

SUPERINTENDENT. Okay. Might need to narrow it down. Is it one of the 'unsuitable use of force ones', or…?

DAISY (*nods at the window*). No, no, it's the… window one.

MANIAC. Which a young anarchist 'accidentally' 'fell from', indeed.

SUPERINTENDENT. Oh yes! That one. Of course. Please do fire away.

MANIAC. Fire away, exactly! Plant the gun on the victim later.

The MANIAC *laughs. The* SUPERINTENDENT *laughs along uneasily. He goes to take a sip of tea but the* MANIAC *takes the mug from him before he has chance.*

Thank you.

He takes a sip of tea and then spits it out.

I'll let that cool down. Here we go then. Let's have a little look at these statements of yours, and see if we can't make sense of all this... in the most blame-effacing way we can.

SUPERINTENDENT. Yes, exactly. That'd be fab...

He opens the file.

MANIAC. Beginning with some facts.

(*To the audience.*) And do pay attention because there will be a test at the end.

(*To the* SUPERINTENDENT.) On the night in question, in this very room, you had a train driver who you believed was responsible for the bombing of a bank a week earlier, agreed?

SUPERINTENDENT. Indeed.

The MANIAC *pins a photo of the Anarchist to the wall.*

MANIAC. Lovely. Now, in this statement he's called an *Anarchist*.

And writes 'anarchist' on the wall.

Why are we calling him that? That's a rather baroque epithet, isn't it?

DAISY. That weren't us. The chief constable said we had to call him that, sir –

MANIAC. I see, a bigger boy made you do it?

DAISY. Well Dame Penelope in this case, but yeah basically –

SUPERINTENDENT. First off we called him a *terrorist*, m'lud, on account of him setting off a bomb, which is absolutely classic terrorist stuff, traditionally, but Dame Penelope was keen for us to call him an 'Anarchist' because as you can see he's uh –

MANIAC. White?

SUPERINTENDENT. Italian. And she was of the opinion that you don't really get Italian terrorists.

MANIAC. Well... Brutus springs to mind, but go on.

SUPERINTENDENT. Plus there's the PR issue of not wanting to scare the public. Which apparently the word 'terrorist' will do, cos it makes people think about big nasty organisations with proper goals and guns and hats and so on, whereas your 'anarchists' are more like lone loonies who just... do stuff... for no reason.

MANIAC. Of course. And what reason could anyone have for wanting to bomb a bank? Perhaps he'd seen that bonuses are back to their highest levels since 2008? Or perhaps he'd just tried to get through to customer services, amirite?

He offers a high-five to JOSEPH.

JOSEPH. Totally.

The SUPERINTENDENT *shoots* JOSEPH *an angry glance.*

MANIAC. Either way, after questioning this *Anarchist* about said bombing, you told the press that there was 'a weight of evidence against him', yes?

SUPERINTENDENT. I did say that, yes, at first. But later on –

MANIAC. Let's stick with 'at first' for now please, Superintendent, we are still in the first act after all –

SUPERINTENDENT. Of course. Please do call me Andy.

During this, the MANIAC *changes the clock to 12:00.*

MANIAC. So, *at first*, Andy, you said that just before midnight, our train-driving Anarchist was 'suddenly seized by a raptus' – your words – and threw himself out of the window, hitting the ground... to death. Now, a raptus? What is that? Isn't that some sort of dinosaur?

The MANIAC *draws a dinosaur on the wall.*

DAISY. What? Is it?

JOSEPH. I believe that's a rapt*or*, m'lud. Velociraptor. Small therapod, about yea big, probably covered in feathers they now think –

SUPERINTENDENT. Stop it.

JOSEPH *immediately stops talking*.

MANIAC. Very good, thank you, Constable, and this is a…?

SUPERINTENDENT. Rapt*us*, m'lud. Also known as 'excited delirium' when we use it in police reports to uh…

MANIAC. Justify lethal use of force.

SUPERINTENDENT. Exactly.

MANIAC. Here we are:

(*Reads*.) 'Raptus. A suicidal impulse induced by a heightened situation that compels otherwise sane people towards unhealthy behaviour.'

SUPERINTENDENT. That. Yeah.

DAISY. In this case, the Anarchist suddenly chucking himself out of the window.

MANIAC. Very unhealthy. Okay, then. Let's see it.

SUPERINTENDENT. The… What's that?

MANIAC. This 'heightened situation' you speak of. This raptus-inducing *mise en scène*. Let's see it.

The MANIAC *starts moving the furniture around*.

SUPERINTENDENT. Oh. Well… How do we…?

MANIAC. Put it on its feet, man. Do a little reconstruction. Give us your famous raptus-making entrance – the one that makes the audience want to commit suicide.

SUPERINTENDENT. I, well, no –

MANIAC. Don't feel bad, Andy, many actors have a similar effect on me –

SUPERINTENDENT. But I wasn't actually here, at that point, it was someone else –

MANIAC. Oh come now, don't pin it on some offstage goon. Play your part, man. Of course you were.

SUPERINTENDENT. Well...

JOSEPH. I'm pretty sure you were, sir –

SUPERINTENDENT. Can you stop butting in, Constable! Jeez Louise! And get me another tea!

JOSEPH. Yes, sir, sorry, sir.

DAISY. And an oat flat white.

JOSEPH *exits.*

MANIAC. Come on, Andy. I bet you know how to make one hell of an entrance.

SUPERINTENDENT. Yes, I, well I do actually...

MANIAC. Of course you do. Please...

SUPERINTENDENT. Right well, it went a little something like this... The Anarchist was over there, and I come in like this, I like to give it a bit of swagger, you know, do my stance...

Demonstrates his walk, ending with an affected stance.

MANIAC. Oh, yes. Bravo!

He addresses DAISY *as though he's the Anarchist.*

SUPERINTENDENT. And I'm like, 'Now look here, you Anarchist... prat, don't you go wasting police time, please...'

MANIAC. No! Boo! Stick to the script, Andy. There's no censorship in here, thank you. Give me your exact words.

SUPERINTENDENT. Yeah, alright, well, in the first statement it's more like, 'Oi!'

MANIAC. Yes! Oi! Go on.

SUPERINTENDENT. 'Oi, fart-face! Stop mucking about and tell us the truth, you little runt.'

MANIAC. 'Runt'? Definitely 'runt'?

SUPERINTENDENT. That's right.

MANIAC. Fair play. Carry on.

SUPERINTENDENT. And I say, 'We've got all the proof we need that it was you that done the other bombing as well.'

MANIAC. What other bombing?

SUPERINTENDENT (*confused*). Well... the one eight months earlier...

MANIAC. Yes, I know, I'm doing the Anarchist's lines to speed things up: 'What other bombing?'

SUPERINTENDENT. Oh right, yes, very good, 'You know what bombing. The one on the train station eight months back. We have proof it was you.'

MANIAC. You're like a young Marlon Brando –

SUPERINTENDENT. Oh, well...

MANIAC. Or an old Daniel Radcliffe.

SUPERINTENDENT. Thank you.

MANIAC. And did you?

SUPERINTENDENT. Did I...?

MANIAC. Have proof it was him?

DAISY *and the* SUPERINTENDENT *are tickled by this idea.*

SUPERINTENDENT. Well, no, I mean –

DAISY. It's an interrogation technique, y'lud –

SUPERINTENDENT. Yes, exactly, it was to lure him into giving himself up –

MANIAC. Yes! Got it. Very clever.

SUPERINTENDENT. But we were fairly sure. I mean for one thing, he was the only train driver working at that station with any links to protest groups, so...

MANIAC. Of course. It's self-evident! The bomb at the train station must have been planted by a train driver, just as all pipe bombs must be made by a plumber and all mail bombs are the work of Postman Pat. Fairly sure indeed! Pah! Come now, gentlemen, I'm here to conduct a serious legal inquiry, not play a game of Pin the Crime On the Donkey! Let's stick to the testimony, shall we? Because here you say, in response to this threat of proof, 'the Anarchist was totally unfazed and smiled sarcastically'. Who said that then?

DAISY. Oh yeah, that was me.

MANIAC. Good man. So he smiled.

The MANIAC *draws a smiley face on the wall.*

And yet, it also says here, 'without doubt his suicidal raptus was caused by his mortal fear of losing his job'.

He draws a sad face on the wall.

So how, I ask you, can he smile and be gripped with fear at the same time?

DAISY. Well, I guess… like this?

DAISY *attempts to smile and look terrified simultaneously. The* MANIAC *sighs.*

MANIAC. God help us.

He pulls them in for a huddle.

Okay look, let's be frank for a second, shall we? I know you're not baking cupcakes in here, fellas. I know the lengths you have to go to to keep society free of all the scum out there. You have to be inventive now and then, give the truth a bit of a bending. I get it, I've seen *Line of Duty*. I'm well aware that it's a facet, if not requirement, of the job.

DAISY. Wicked, cheers.   SUPERINTENDENT. Thank
                                   you very much, m'lud.

MANIAC. So what did you say to shit him up? His train-driving career's gone off the rails, Elon Musk's about to release self-driving trains, he'll never work again… and he loses it and lunges for the window?

DAISY. Well no, if I may, y'lud, the out-of-the-window bit wasn't as quick as all that. I did do some further questioning myself –

MANIAC. Of course you did. I'm so sorry, I'm not trying to cut your part.

(*Reads.*) So, according to the report, you exited, and then re-entered and, after pausing for dramatic effect, said… well you do it, they're your lines. Imagine Andy's the Anarchist –

DAISY. Right, sure, just a sec.

He shakes out his hands and feet. And clears his throat.

MANIAC. Oh lovely, yes, please do warm up.

DAISY. I did a bit of acting at school.

He exits and re-enters, miming smoking a cigarette.

'I've just had a call from Scotland Yard.'

MANIAC. In your own voice, probably.

DAISY. Sure, yeah, if you want.

He exits again. And re-enters.

'I've just had a call from Scotland Yard. And it's bad news, bozo. Your dancer flatmate, or should I say, co-conspirator, has confessed to the bombing on the bank.'

MANIAC. Aha! Wonderful. And was that true?

DAISY. He did live with a dancer, yeah –

MANIAC. About the confession?

DAISY. Oh. No, obviously not.

MANIAC. Of course. Silly me. And how did he respond?

DAISY. Well whatever it says there…

(*Reads.*) 'He gloomily begged for a cigarette and lit it…'

MANIAC. And then jumped out of the window?

SUPERINTENDENT. Well, no, not right away.

MANIAC. Ah. Not *right away*. But you did say 'right away', didn't you? In this first version?

SUPERINTENDENT. We did, yes, annoyingly.

MANIAC. And you told the press and the TV news people that just before his tragic self-defenestration, the Anarchist declared that he felt 'trapped'. Is that right? Trapped? Not 'entrapped'?

DAISY. Is there a difference?

MANIAC. Maybe not to you –

SUPERINTENDENT. Trapped. I said he said trapped.

MANIAC. And what else did you say?

SUPERINTENDENT. Well... that his alibi, that he was playing cards by the canal with some builder friends all afternoon, had been exposed as bollocks.

MANIAC. And so, with his bollocks exposed, you concluded that '*therefore* the Anarchist was heavily implicated in both the bombing in the bank and the bombing in the station some eight months earlier'. And that his suicidal dive from the window was 'a clear indication of guilt'.

The MANIAC *writes 'guilt'.*

SUPERINTENDENT. At the time we did say that, yes –

During this the MANIAC *writes 'psycho', 'naturally' and a then a halo above the photo of the Anarchist.*

MANIAC. And you called him 'a psycho... a menace to society' and yet, and yet, just two weeks later, you then declared that the evidence against him was 'naturally' – that word again, 'naturally' – insubstantial and that not only was the Anarchist 'in all probability innocent', but that he was in fact 'a nice guy'.

SUPERINTENDENT. Yes, I admitted that we made a bit of a... mistake.

MANIAC. A *mistake*? Ordering red wine with fish is a *mistake*. Buying clothes from River Island is a *mistake*. You bring in an innocent man, hold him for over the legal limit, tell him he's going to get sacked, that his alibi's collapsed, that you've got the proof you need to bang him up for bombing the station *and* the bank, *then*, mincing his mind even more, that his dancer flatmate's confessed to being more la bomber than *la bamba* and that he should just save everyone a lot of bother and confess. I mean, call me crazy, but it's no wonder that the guy gets seized by a raptus and jumps out the window! He was probably carted off by a whole flock of rapti. Because from where I'm sitting, fellas, this so-called suicide was aided, abetted, created, curated by you.

SUPERINTENDENT. But... you said yourself, m'lud, we have to tweak the truth when interrogating, wind people up a bit. It's not our fault he was so fragile upstairs that he couldn't take a wee bit of needling –

MANIAC. A bit of needling? A stitch-up, I think you mean! Yes or no, did you have any proof that he'd lied about his alibi?

SUPERINTENDENT. Not... no –

MANIAC. And, yes or no, are there two or three builders who played cards with him that day who can back up his story?

DAISY. Well... yeah, there will be.

MANIAC. And yes or no, had this dancer actually confessed? Because it's not in the file...

DAISY. No, we made that up.

MANIAC (*grabbing his heart*). Oh my! Oh mercy me oh my! Oh, this is too much! You two really ought to be writers – you're wasted in the force, I tell you. You guys should write the next Marvel franchise. You'll have more than enough time, of course, when you're in prison.

SUPERINTENDENT. When we're in what sorry where...?

MANIAC. What's the matter? Don't like that? Cos that's what's coming, baby – I kid you not. Scotland Yard have overwhelming proof of your gross negligence and want to make an example of you. The Home Secretary herself is demanding that Tweedledum and Tweedledumber here are sent down for somewhere between ages and always.

Beat. They stare at him.

SUPERINTENDENT. No...

MANIAC. No?

DAISY. I thought they were sorting it out?

MANIAC. Well you thought wrong, kiddo. It's your cocks on the block now. Don't be too minty, I blame the politics really. Ninety-five per cent of crimes go unsolved after the cuts of the last decade, you see? Honestly, these student snowflakes suddenly demanding to 'defund the police'. We were doing it before it was even cool! And lo and behold, what's the result? Corners get cut, egos get bruised, suspects get killed, Scotland Yard need to serve up a scapegoat curry and you two are the cops to cop it –

SUPERINTENDENT. But… specifically us two?

MANIAC. Specifically.

DAISY. This is bullshit!

SUPERINTENDENT. Big old bullshit!

The MANIAC *pulls them in for a huddle.*

MANIAC. Here's an old proverb for you: 'The landowner sets his dogs on the peasants, if the peasants complain to the king, the landowner, to make amends, shoots his dogs.' I hope that helps.

DAISY. Not really. Who are we?

MANIAC. The dogs. And sadly, I've been sent by the king.

SUPERINTENDENT. This is a set-up!

MANIAC. And I hope the irony isn't lost on you. I think most people will be very pleased with this outcome.

DAISY. Right, yeah, starting with some of the wankers here!

SUPERINTENDENT. And the press! Imagine the horrid stuff they'll print about us!

DAISY. Oh they'll lap it up. Evil, lying, violent Met scum –

SUPERINTENDENT. I try extremely hard not to be any of those things!

DAISY. The corruption, the cover-ups, the toxic culture –

SUPERINTENDENT. I've never even posted anything on the WhatsApp group!

DAISY. The racism, the misogyny…

SUPERINTENDENT. I actually like Meghan Markle –

DAISY. I can't go to prison!

SUPERINTENDENT. Thirty years of loyal service and this is how they repay me!

DAISY. Look at me, I'm a pretty boy.

SUPERINTENDENT. I only kept doing this bloody job for the pension!

DAISY. They'll tear me a new one in there!

SUPERINTENDENT. My brother'll fucking love this.

DAISY. What do we do, y'lud?

SUPERINTENDENT. This is all his Christmases come at once.

DAISY. Please?!

MANIAC. I don't know! Why are you asking me?

DAISY. You're a judge, you must have some idea –

SUPERINTENDENT. Yes, you have to help us –

DAISY. If you were in this position, what would you do?

MANIAC. If I were your position…?

SUPERINTENDENT. What would you do?

DAISY. Please!

MANIAC. Well… in your position…

SUPERINTENDENT. Yes?

DAISY. Tell us –

SUPERINTENDENT. Please tell us!

The MANIAC *opens the window.*

MANIAC. I'd throw myself out of the window.

SUPERINTENDENT. Yes! Sorry, what?

MANIAC. You asked for my advice and there it is. The humiliation you face is indeed unbearable. You will be disowned by your family, devoured by society, disgraced by history, forever filed in the fat folder marked 'pricks'. If I were you I'd end it all now. What are you waiting for?

DAISY. I don't think I can though –

MANIAC. You don't need to, the raptus will do it for you.

SUPERINTENDENT. Now hang on a sec –

MANIAC. Why give any more of your time and energy to this bastard planet! Take your revenge, headbutt it from a great height!

SUPERINTENDENT. But surely there's still hope?

The MANIAC *begins to guide them towards the window.*

MANIAC. Nope. No hope. Abandon all hope ye who enter here. Hope has flown out of the window; if you jump now you can maybe catch it on the way down.

DAISY. No please, anything but that –

MANIAC. Your best years are behind you, I promise, you'll never get a better part than this...

SUPERINTENDENT. Well don't... What are you doing – ?

MANIAC. It's not me, it's the raptus. Hurrah, here comes raptus the liberator, ready to set you free...

The MANIAC *guides them up onto the windowsill.*

DAISY. No, please...   MANIAC. Give in to the
                                                raptus!

JOSEPH *enters. He holds two mugs.*

JOSEPH. One tea and one oat flattie...

(*Seeing them on the sill.*) Is everything alright?

They all freeze. The MANIAC *lets go of them.*

MANIAC. Yes of course! Haha, it's all in hand. Get down from there, you'll do yourself a mischief.

The MANIAC *pulls* DAISY *and the* SUPERINTENDENT *down.*

Apologies for this rather Jacobean tableau, Constable, I'm afraid the two officers had been temporarily seized by a raptus.

SUPERINTENDENT. Yes… What, was I?

JOSEPH. A raptus?

MANIAC. Yes, they were trying to throw themselves out of the window.

JOSEPH. What? *They* were?

MANIAC. It was only a bit of fun. Don't tell the press, there's a love.

JOSEPH. Yes, no, never.

DAISY. No, it were him! He was pulling my arm –

MANIAC. I was pulling your leg! You should have seen them, they were so wild with fear that they totally fell for it and very nearly *from it*. Oh cheer up, you two. Look at their glum little faces, Constable! They look like the headmaster's caught them fiddling with themselves!

JOSEPH (*laughs*). Yeah! Or with each other!

SUPERINTENDENT. Watch your bloody mouth, you!

JOSEPH. I'm so sorry sir, I meant, I meant, there's nothing wrong with it. It's a free country.

JOSEPH *passes the* SUPERINTENDENT *and* DAISY *their hot drinks.*

MANIAC. Not any more it's not! Keep up, man! Have you not read the new Public Order Act?

The MANIAC *takes the tea from the* SUPERINTENDENT.

Thank you. Now come on, chin up, I'd like to put this behind me, as the actress said to the so on and so forth.

SUPERINTENDENT. Well that's easy for you to say... I think there was a moment there when I was actually going to do it.

DAISY. And me. I had that.

MANIAC. Aha! You see, gentlemen, the power of the raptus? And who, I ask you, would have been to blame for setting it off?

SUPERINTENDENT. Well the bastard powers-that-be, like you said. Pinning all their shit on us, getting all antsy when some Johnny Foreigner gets caught in the crossfire.

MANIAC. No, no, far from it. The fault would have been all mine.

SUPERINTENDENT. Well... Really, why?

MANIAC. Because I made it up. It's not true.

SUPERINTENDENT. You mean... Scotland Yard aren't hanging us out to dry?

MANIAC. Holding you up as heroes more like.

DAISY. But what about the Home Secretary?

MANIAC. Oh, she couldn't give a shit! She's down in Dover with her BB gun trying to pop any dinghies crossing the Channel.

SUPERINTENDENT. You're not pulling our leg again?

MANIAC. Of course not! Everyone's right behind you.

DAISY. Oh thank fuck.

MANIAC. As if the government suddenly care about some innocent immigrant all of a sudden? That's one less on the spreadsheet, isn't it? One less benefits tourist for the tabloids to moan about. It's their own fault for not speaking English, it's their own fault for living in a tower block, it's their own fault for going out in short skirts. I made it all up. Even the proverb. No landowner has ever shot a dog to satisfy a peasant, I assure you.

SUPERINTENDENT. So, sorry, forgive me for being a bit dim –

MANIAC. Of course, you can't help that –

SUPERINTENDENT. Thank you, but if we weren't being thrown to the wolves after all, why did you make us go through that whole… pantomime?

MANIAC. 'Pantomime'?! How dare you? Do you see any pirate ships or former *Love Island* contestants anywhere? Do you see any hard-up children's entertainers from the 1970s who are yet to be investigated by Operation Yewtree? Pantomime, indeed!

SUPERINTENDENT. Sorry, I didn't mean pantomime –

MANIAC. I was employing a technique used by the judiciary to demonstrate to the police that this 'false scenario' method of interrogation is at best naughty and at worst criminal.

SUPERINTENDENT. I see. So you do still think we had a hand in the Anarchist's falling out of the window?

MANIAC. I do. I think you had *a* hand *in*, if not *four* hands *on* the guy. Exactly as I demonstrated to you just now.

SUPERINTENDENT. Because I wasn't actually here when he fell out, was I, Constable?

DAISY. Nor me. I weren't here either.

JOSEPH. Oh yeah no, that's right, yes, they'd just that moment left, so they couldn't have pushed him.

MANIAC. Well I don't know, there is the 'long arm of the law', isn't there?

SUPERINTENDENT. No no, I mean –

MANIAC. Anyway, you were the ones who lit the fuse in the guy, it hardly matters if you scarpered directly before he went off.

SUPERINTENDENT. No but, sorry, there's been a mix-up. The constable's talking about the first version, where we left 'directly before', and I'm talking about the second version, where I'd been gone for some time…

The MANIAC *flicks through the pages.*

MANIAC. Ah yes! The second draft! A bit of a rewrite after the producers have given their notes –

SUPERINTENDENT. Not a rewrite, really, a correction –

MANIAC. Of course. So, come on, what's been corrected?

The SUPERINTENDENT *nods to* DAISY*, who guides the* MANIAC *through the pages.*

DAISY. Right, well we changed –

SUPERINTENDENT. No –

DAISY. *Properly remembered*, the time of the interrogation, when we told the Anarchist the not-strictly-true stuff about his alibi falling apart –

MANIAC. I see. So when was that then?

DAISY. Well in the first version it's around midnight, directly before the whole jumping bit, but in the second version it's actually at eight.

The MANIAC *changes the hands of the clock to 8:00.*

MANIAC. You've brought the jump forward four hours! Now why have you done that?

DAISY. No, no, the jump was still at midnight, we didn't change that –

SUPERINTENDENT. Well we couldn't, there was a journalist in the courtyard who saw the Anarchist hit the pavement, so that's very much… set in stone.

MANIAC. Along with his front teeth, I imagine. Right, so, according to this second gospel, the Anarchist's moment of existential crisis, as induced by your porkiepies, took place at around eight, and yet his suicide was at midnight. Which obviously leads me to ask: what happened to this *sudden* raptus? It's suddenly not very sudden, is it, if it took four hours to get here? Did it get stuck on the District line? Did it stop off to watch *Avatar: Way of Water*? I might remind you that this whole case hinges on this 'raptus' business – so you can't chuck that out the window as well.

SUPERINTENDENT. We haven't.

MANIAC. Yes you have.

SUPERINTENDENT. No, no, we want to show that there was still a raptus, but because it happened *much* later, it can't have been our fault.

MANIAC. Yes! Of course! You're right! Very well done, both of you, you're an absolute credit to the uniform.

The MANIAC *shakes their hands passionately.*

DAISY. Cheers.   SUPERINTENDENT. Thank
                                        you, m'lud.

MANIAC. It can't have been your doing if it took the guy four hours to act upon it. Not even Sting takes that long to climax.

SUPERINTENDENT. Exactly. So we're innocent.

MANIAC. As innocent as an Innocent Smoothie made from the internal organs of Bambi. I mean, it does mean that we have no idea why our Anarchist train-driver friend took his own life when he did, but who cares? The main thing is, as ever, that the police are in the clear.

SUPERINTENDENT. I'm so glad you see it that way.

MANIAC. But of course.

(*Then*.) So, the key thing to put beyond all doubt is that after this hiatus of four hours the Anarchist had fully recovered from what the last judge described as his 'psychological collapse'.

DAISY. Yes, we did that. That's in the second statement, look.

He shows him.

'He had recovered.'

During the next, the MANIAC *leads* JOSEPH *to the desk, takes out a typewriter from his bag and sets it in front of him.*

MANIAC. We need a bit more than that, you hunky numpty! Jesus wept. We need evidence. Details that make it as clear as our collective conscience that when you two left the room,

our anarchic chum was in good spirits. And his later suicide
bid – a winning bid as it turned out – was in spite of your
efforts and not because of them. So... how did you do it?

They think.

JOSEPH. I gave him some gum.

MANIAC. Good man. What flavour?

JOSEPH. Cherry menthol.

MANIAC. Punchy. Get it down then.

The MANIAC *sits* JOSEPH *at the typewriter.*

JOSEPH. Right, yes.

JOSEPH *starts typing.*

MANIAC. Superintendent? Any ideas?

SUPERINTENDENT. No, I wasn't actually here.

MANIAC. At a delicate moment like this, you must have been!

SUPERINTENDENT. No, I don't think so –

MANIAC. Think harder.

SUPERINTENDENT. Uh...   MANIAC. Harder still.
    no, I –

SUPERINTENDENT. Oh I see. Yes, sorry I was –

MANIAC. Of course you were. And is it not fair to say that,
given how gloomy the Anarchist was feeling after the
interrogation, you and the detective here were rather moved.

DAISY. Yeah. And the rest. I was well moved.

MANIAC (*writes*). As, I assume, were you, Superintendent – a
man so famously soppy that his favourite film is *Watership
Down*, is it not?

SUPERINTENDENT. Ugh, yeah, I mean, it can be, I like a
rabbit...

MANIAC. Exactly. So you were...

SUPERINTENDENT. Deeply moved.

MANIAC. Correct! So much so that I bet you gave him a wee pat on his shoulder –

SUPERINTENDENT. Uh… no, I don't think so –

MANIAC. A small, paternal gesture…

SUPERINTENDENT. Um, well… maybe, I don't remember –

MANIAC. Those big beautiful hands are built for patting. Of course you did, tell me you did!

JOSEPH. He did. I saw him do it.

SUPERINTENDENT. Well, I mean, if he saw it then maybe –

MANIAC. And then that pat became a tiny hug –

SUPERINTENDENT. No. It didn't.

MANIAC. Didn't it?

SUPERINTENDENT. No fucking way.

MANIAC. Just a brief squeeze to let him know that he's not alone, that you feel his pain –

SUPERINTENDENT. No, look, I'm sorry to disappoint you but I don't go round feeling other blokes'… pain, not ever. There's nothing wrong with it, but it's very much not my bag.

MANIAC. Well you do disappoint me. And do you know why? Because this man wasn't just an Anarchist. He wasn't just an Italian. He was a train driver. And do you know why trains are significant here? I'll tell you. Because they are a direct link, an iron rail, back to your childhood. Back when you were innocent. Before beer and bills and anti-discrimination legislation came along and ruined everything. Before the internet, when the world was mysterious and vast, and there was no greater sight than that streak of steel shimmering across the horizon, and no greater sound than the growing growl of the distant locomotive. Because you are men, and once you were boys. And every time you step on board a train, no matter where it is headed, you are in some small way… going home.

SUPERINTENDENT. Yes, I mean, that's a bit OTT but –

MANIAC. Surely you had toy trains as a boy, Andy? Surely you did?

SUPERINTENDENT. Well, yes, I had a small train set that we put out in the shed, you know, a Hornby one. I had a steam train, an intercity diesel obviously –

MANIAC. And did it go 'toot toot'?

SUPERINTENDENT. I think there was a built-in tooting function yes…

MANIAC. Please… let me hear you do it…

SUPERINTENDENT. Uh… *toot toot.*

The MANIAC *claps his hands together.*

MANIAC. Do you know, when you toot-tooted there, your little eyes lit up, they really did. Of course you felt a deep bond with this man, Andy, your unconscious mind associated him with your train set. With the *toot toot.* Of course you gave him a hug.

The SUPERINTENDENT *weighs this up.*

JOSEPH. I saw him do that as well. It was quite a deep hug.

MANIAC. You see? We have a witness.

SUPERINTENDENT. Well… yes, alright, a manly hug though. My fists were closed.

MANIAC. But of course.

DAISY. What was I doing?

MANIAC. Well you lit his cigarette for him, didn't you?

DAISY. Oh yeah, I did actually.

MANIAC. And when he gloomily declared that he felt 'trapped', you squatted down next to him –

DAISY. Great, yeah, I love a squat.

MANIAC. And said, 'If you are as innocent, as you claim…'

DAISY. 'If you are as innocent as you claim…'

MANIAC. 'Then I promise you with my all my heart...'

DAISY. 'Then I promise you with all my heart', yup...

MANIAC. Well go on, you're the one that fucking said it –

DAISY. Right, yeah, 'with all my heart that we will... make sure... that...'

MANIAC. 'You will be – '

DAISY. 'You will be...'

MANIAC. 'Given your – '

DAISY. 'Given your... compensation'?

MANIAC. 'Freedom.'

DAISY. 'Freedom', yes! Great.

MANIAC. And then, of course... you sang.

SUPERINTENDENT. What? Sang?

MANIAC. Of course you did. Having forged such unbreakable bonds of kinship, the only logical thing to do was burst into song. But what was it? 'Bohemian Rhapsody'? 'We Found Love in a Hopeless Place'? Maybe something Italian. Something that reminded him of the old country. 'Nessun Dorma'? Or, better still, 'Bella Ciao', the anthem of Italian anti-fascism in the 1940s, recently co-opted by protesters in Greece and Wall Street and even sung at the funeral of the dear writer of this very play...

DAISY. What? What do you mean 'play'?

SUPERINTENDENT. No, I'm sorry, m'lud, I really can't go with you on that.

MANIAC. Well that's because I haven't taught it to you yet.

SUPERINTENDENT. We did not sing. No way, José. Didn't happen. The patting, the hugging, fine, but this song business is old-school horseshit, pardon my French. We did not have a sudden sing-song in here, and I won't start saying we did.

MANIAC. Is that right?

SUPERINTENDENT. It is.

MANIAC. Well... up yours then.

DAISY. What?

MANIAC. You heard me, sonny. Up your arse. I've tried my best here, boys, I've sweated blood trying to massage this mess into something on-message and this is what I get. You won't sing. Fine. I will happily present the facts exactly as you've explained them to me. And you know where that'll get you? The clink, Strangeways, a lengthy stay at His Majesty's pleasure. You won't sing? Then you can sod off to Sing Sing.

SUPERINTENDENT. Well there's no need to be like that, m'lud –

MANIAC. Isn't there? You're driving me mad here, lads. First you give me one version, then half an hour later I get the detective's cut, the superintendent's cut, ChatGPT's cut... it's an absolute multiverse of madness! I mean, heavens to Betsy, have you forgotten your training? Police collusion only works if you all sing from the same hymn sheet. First you tell the media that there's no transcript of the interview with the Anarchist, because there wasn't time to get it down, and then two or three of them miraculously drop from the sky all saying different things. Do you know how this looks?

SUPERINTENDENT. Bad?

MANIAC. It does look bad, yes. It makes the public think you're liars. It makes them think you're self-serving, corrupt fascists, but that's not the even the worst part.

SUPERINTENDENT. Well... Is it not?

MANIAC. They think you lack respect. For society, for the media, for them. Who pays your wages, mate?

He points to the audience.

They do. That lot. And I'm not asking you to say thank you, I'm not even asking for a receipt, I'm just asking you to make an effort. Yes, your version of the facts is inconsistent and muddled and demands a suspension if not expulsion of disbelief, but worse than that, it lacks heart. It lacks humanity. That's what we're looking for here. Sympathetic characters: people we can relate to. They'll forgive everything if you give them that. The gaping holes in your plot, the clunky dialogue, the fact that only one per cent of complaints against police officers result in misconduct proceedings, they'll let it all slide if they thought there were real people under the uniform. That you're flawed angels, not trained apes. And if they thought, in a brief snatch of sympathy for this poor, innocent Anarchist, that you had somehow overcome the social divisions of class, race, profession, position, everything, and sang... in the name of unity and empathy... oh boys, oh lads oh lads, I promise you, there would not be a dry seat in the house. They would toast your health around every dinner table in the land, proud to call themselves your countrymen. So I beg you, for the Anarchist's sake, for the inquiry's sake, for your sake, for God's sake... sing!

The MANIAC *begins to sing. The* POLICEMEN *slowly start to join in, their singing timid and off-key.*

Una mattina mi son svegliato,
o bella ciao, bella ciao, bella ciao ciao ciao!
Una mattina mi son svegliato
e ho trovato l'invasor.

O partigiano portami via,
o bella ciao, bella ciao, bella ciao ciao ciao
o partigiano portami via
che mi sento di morir.

As the POLICEMEN *start to memorise the lyrics, the* MANIAC *turns to the audience.*

By all means go and get a drink, use the facilities, et cetera, sounds like this might take a wee while...

Interval.

ACT TWO

The singing resumes. We see the progress that the POLICEMEN
have made. They are now singing in a beautiful three-part
harmony, the song has become very passionate and doleful.
The MANIAC *lowers the blind. The sun sets. It is now night.*

ALL.

> E se io muoio da partigiano,
> o bella ciao, bella ciao, bella ciao ciao ciao,
> e se io muoio da partigiano
> tu mi devi seppellir.

> Seppellire lassù in montagna,
> o bella ciao, bella ciao, bella ciao ciao ciao,
> seppellire lassù in montagna
> sotto l'ombra di un bel fior.

> E le genti che passeranno,
> o bella ciao, bella ciao, bella ciao ciao ciao,
> e le genti che passeranno
> mi diranno 'Che bel fior!'

> Questo è il fiore del partigiano,
> o bella ciao, bella ciao, bella ciao ciao ciao,
> questo è il fiore del partigiano
> morto per la libertà!

The MANIAC *applauds, moved, delighted.*

MANIAC. *Bravi, bravi! Addesso sí, che ci siamo. A questo
punto nessuno potrá mettere in dubbio che...*

(*To the audience.*) ...but what am I saying, all that Italian
made me forget we'd hired a translator!

(*To the cops.*) So, as that performance puts beyond doubt, at
this point our Anarchist, and indeed anyone lucky enough to
witness such a sublime sing-song, was in a state of total
tranquillity, was he not?

DAISY. I reckon he was even happy.

MANIAC. Well he probably felt right at home with you guys! God knows his protest groups are mostly made up of undercover cops, this will have felt very familiar.

SUPERINTENDENT. Exactly. Point is, any trauma caused by our... alternative facts during questioning had been completely cleansed.

MANIAC. As though his brain had been bathed in bleach. Therefore... no raptus. That comes later. When was it again?

DAISY. Midnight.

The MANIAC *changes the time on the clock.*

MANIAC. Midnight. How apt. For now, gentlemen, it is time for part two of our story, the death of the Anarchist itself, the grizzly business of our title. We must now prove not only that you didn't cause it, but that you did everything in your power to prevent it. So... what happened?

SUPERINTENDENT. Well, as I recall –

MANIAC. No! You do not recall anything, you were not here at midnight. Remember?

SUPERINTENDENT. Apologies. My mind was elsewhere –

MANIAC. As was your body. Tell us what happened, Detective.

DAISY. Yeah, I'm pretty sure I wasn't here either actually...

MANIAC. Oh for the love of a good woman, you can't both go missing. Or am I relying solely the testimony of this gormless con... stable?

JOSEPH. Can do if you like –

SUPERINTENDENT. No. No way. Daisy was here. Weren't you?

DAISY. Alright, yeah, I was, I just nipped out straight after is all...

MANIAC. Okay, well pre-nipping, how many of you were in the room?

SUPERINTENDENT. I'm a bit nippy now actually –

DAISY. So... there was me, three officers and a sergeant from plain-clothes.

JOSEPH. And me.

MANIAC. Six of you! Why? What were you doing? Spin the Bottle? Soggy Biscuit?

DAISY. Well no, we were still interrogating him.

SUPERINTENDENT. Anyone else a bit nippy?

MANIAC. After four hours?! What is there left to ask? What's your star sign? Do you fold the loo roll or scrunch it up?

(*Sings*.) 'Getting to know you, getting to know all about you.'

DAISY. Well it was as bit different now, y'lud, by this point the interrogation had become more, you know... jokey.

SUPERINTENDENT. Close the window, Constable.

JOSEPH *stands heads over to the window.*

MANIAC. Sorry? *Jokey?*

DAISY. It was, weren't it, Constable?

JOSEPH (*stops*). Oh, yeah, it was actually –

DAISY. And it's in the inquiry, look, the first judge made a note of it.

The MANIAC *leafs through the paper.*

MANIAC. Let me see... by Jove, he's right! Here it is in black and white. 'The later interrogation was somewhat jokey.' What are we talking? Impressions? Puns? Recreating a few *Two Ronnies* sketches? 'Four candles!'

DAISY. Well no, but –

MANIAC. Talk about unsuitable use of farce!

JOSEPH. The detective can be pretty funny actually... not always on purpose but still...

DAISY. Cheers. What?

JOSEPH. He was mucking around a bit, you know, telling some jokes…

MANIAC. But of course, you were doing one of your routines…

(To the empty chair.) I say I say I say, did you hear the one about the copper accused of brutally assaulting his suspects? No, what's the punchline? This is!

The MANIAC *mimes beating the suspect, laughing wildly.*

DAISY. I didn't hit the guy, yeah?

MANIAC. Nor did I, there's no one there. This explains everything, Detective. When I was living in a charming little squat in East London a few years back I remember some local lads being regularly interrogated by some equally hilarious bobbies, and I see now that the piercing howls that woke me in the night were merely bouts of laughter. It was the sound of sides splitting. 'Ha, Officer, please, you're killing me here… stop, please stop, I can't breathe!'

SUPERINTENDENT. Well now, m'lud, of course some officers will get a bit physical now and then. Some interrogations can get a bit, sure, tasty –

MANIAC. Tasty! They're bloody delicious these days. Use of force has jumped nearly eighty per cent in the last five years!

SUPERINTENDENT. And some cases will sadly require a bit of targeted rough-and-tumble –

MANIAC. Targeted on young black men mainly. It's five times more common in fact –

SUPERINTENDENT. But that's going to happen in this line of work! We're working to urgent deadlines, with fine margins, and obviously from time to time, patience wears thin, tempers run high and – Constable! Close the fucking window! How many times?

JOSEPH. Yes, sir, sorry, sir.

He does so. Beat.

SUPERINTENDENT. I get ratty when I'm cold.

MANIAC. Of course. And you're dead right, it has got a bit
chilly suddenly…

DAISY. That's because the sun's gone down.

MANIAC. Oh bravo, Detective. I can see how you got your job
with effortless deduction like that. Wonderful to witness, it
really is. Although, of course, on the night in question, the
sun didn't go down, did it?

DAISY. It… You what?

MANIAC. Think about it. There you all were, at midnight,
interrogating away, hilariously, with the window completely
akimbo. So evidently it wasn't cold. Which, if we apply the
detective's deductive genius, would mean that the sun hadn't
set.

SUPERINTENDENT. Ah no, it was just opened for a moment,
to clear the air –

MANIAC. You weren't here –

SUPERINTENDENT. I imagine. I imagine it was –

JOSEPH. It was, yes.

DAISY. It was well smoky in here.

JOSEPH. The Anarchist smoked! We said so in the first version.

DAISY. Right, yeah, that'll be why!

MANIAC. So you opened the window *and* the blinds?

DAISY. Er… yeah, why not?

MANIAC. At midnight? In December? When the icy wind
chills you to the pips? When families must decide between
hypothermia and bankruptcy? How did you avoid catching
pneumonia? I presume you were all sporting full-length seal
skins?

JOSEPH. No, just the uniforms.

MANIAC. Just that polyester two-piece?

JOSEPH. It's a woollen blend…

DAISY. And it weren't *that* cold.

The MANIAC *looks through the notes.*

MANIAC. It says it was minus-three.

DAISY. Yeah well… whatever.

MANIAC. Oh 'whateva'? Of course.

DAISY. It didn't bother us.

MANIAC. I see. And why was that? Are you all cold-blooded perhaps? Are you examples of David Icke's so-called Reptilian Elite? Because that would explain a lot –

SUPERINTENDENT. What are you driving at, m'lud? If you don't mind me asking? I mean, you say you're here to help us –

MANIAC. I am –

SUPERINTENDENT. And yet all you've done is pick holes in everything we're saying. Yes, the window was open for a bit. Why? Because it was. And yeah, it was a bit parky, but we're grown men and we can deal with it.

DAISY. You weren't here –

SUPERINTENDENT. *They* can deal with it. And they did –

MANIAC. That's all I wanted to hear, Superintendent. That'll work fine. Forgive me for being pernickety, but I want to make sure that our version of events is cast-iron.

He writes.

Why was the window open? Because these coppers… are fucking nails.

SUPERINTENDENT. Right. So we can move on.

MANIAC. We can. Let us go then, you and I, to when our Anarchist is spread out against the sky.

SUPERINTENDENT. The jump, you mean?

MANIAC. I do. So, at midnight, our Anarchist chum is seized by this raptus, of origin unknown, given that you lot definitely didn't cause it, and rises from his chair and after a short sprint – hang on, who gave him the leg-up?

DAISY. The what?

MANIAC. I assume someone was stationed here to provide a launch pad? Or wheeled in a springboard? No?

DAISY. No, I mean, we didn't help him –

MANIAC. No? Because it is rather high.

DAISY. He was a good jumper.

MANIAC. Clearly. What was the technique? Fosbury flop? Scissors kick?

DAISY. Just... head-first –

MANIAC. Superman-style. Sure. Well, if he was unassisted, that would be an Olympian feat of athleticism.

SUPERINTENDENT. Of course he was *unassisted*. What are you trying to say?

MANIAC. Nothing, Superintendent, back in your box. I am simply pointing out that we have a five-foot-three, chain-smoking Italian who, with no ladder or jetpack at his disposal, is able to launch himself out of this window with such velocity that the six policemen in the room at the time, some only inches away, were unable to stop him...

DAISY. It was well sudden, though, y'lud! He slipped right through us like a greased gimp.

JOSEPH. He did, yeah. I only just managed to get him by the foot.

The MANIAC *spins and stares at* JOSEPH, *excited.*

MANIAC. Say that again!

The SUPERINTENDENT *is suddenly on high alert.*

JOSEPH. I... only just managed to get him by the foot.

The MANIAC *shakes his hand.*

MANIAC. Ha! See how my Paxman-esque pedantry bears fruit! You got him by the foot?

JOSEPH. I... think so. Is that... good?

MANIAC. It is.

DAISY. He did then. He definitely did.

JOSEPH. I made a statement about it. The shoe came off in my hand and he carried on falling to the ground –

MANIAC. Aha! The shoe remained!

JOSEPH. I should have got his ankle really –

MANIAC. No matter, the shoe is the thing! The shoe is the irrefutable proof of your ardent efforts to save him.

The MANIAC *draws a shoe on the wall.*

SUPERINTENDENT. Yes exactly! Terrific work, Constable… what's your name again?

JOSEPH. Joseph, sir.

SUPERINTENDENT. Well done, Joseph.

The MANIAC *looks at the papers on the desk.*

JOSEPH. Thank you, sir. I knew in that moment I had to act, instinct just took over and –

SUPERINTENDENT. Yes alright, that'll do.

MANIAC. Hang on… something's not right here… unless, did the Anarchist by any chance have three shoes?

DAISY. What? Three shoes?

MANIAC. Only reason I ask is that one shoe we know was yanked off by the constable here, that was recorded in the first inquiry, and yet, witness reports and photos from the scene of the splat confirm that the Anarchist was, without doubt, wearing two shoes.

SUPERINTENDENT. Oh. Shit.

MANIAC. Indeed. Unless… the constable was so fleet that he was able to race to the window on the floor below and put the shoe back on the Anarchist's foot as he passed by.

SUPERINTENDENT. Well that's just silly.

MANIAC. You're right, I'm sorry for lowering the tone. The only logical explanation here is, of course, that the Anarchist was a tri-ped.

SUPERINTENDENT. A tri-ped. Like a... three-footer?

MANIAC. Exactly. He was an Anarchist after all, and what could me more anarchic than having three legs? All the better for anar-kicking you with.

JOSEPH. Ha! That's funny.

MANIAC. I'm here all week.

DAISY. Yeah, well we need a proper explanation for this or it looks like we're just making shit up.

SUPERINTENDENT. Which we're not.

MANIAC. And I might just have it! Try this on for size. Maybe one of his shoes was too big.

SUPERINTENDENT. Why?

MANIAC. Well because... he didn't try it on for size, it doesn't matter why, let's just say it is –

SUPERINTENDENT. Alright, alright –

MANIAC. And, given that he didn't have an insole, he deployed another, narrow shoe to go inside the big one – an *in-shoe* if you like – and then wore the big one on top of that.

The MANIAC *draws a shoe over another shoe.*

DAISY. Two shoes on the same foot?

MANIAC. Why not? We've had a terrorist who put a bomb in his shoe, haven't we? This guy's just put a shoe in his shoe.

DAISY. That's fucking ridiculous.

MANIAC. Exactly. It's perfectly in keeping with most explanations given for a deaths in police custody... get it down, Constable.

JOSEPH types away. The telephone suddenly rings.

Oh how exciting. A phone call! Do you think this is some vital new piece of evidence or just someone trying to reach the box office?

DAISY *answers it.*

DAISY. Y'ello, fourth floor. Dan Daisy speaking.

(*To the* SUPERINTENDENT.) It's the desk sergeant, sir, saying there's a journalist here to see you.

SUPERINTENDENT. Oh shit the bed, frankly! Yes, I forgot she was coming. What's her name again? Phelan or something?

DAISY. I'll check.

(*To the phone*.) Is she Phelan, right?

(*To the* SUPERINTENDENT.) Apparently she's fine.

(*To the phone*.) Is her name Phelan?

(*To the* SUPERINTENDENT.) Yeah, that's her.

MANIAC. Fine. Send her up!

DAISY (*to the phone*). Yeah, tell her to –

The SUPERINTENDENT *snatches the receiver.*

SUPERINTENDENT. No! Stop! I'll tell her I'm busy, we'll have to postpone –

MANIAC. Oh, no, don't let yourself look incompetent for my sake, Andy.

SUPERINTENDENT. Incompetent, what? No, I'm not.

MANIAC. Exactly. But this hack doesn't know that. You miss your interview and she'll paint you as some hapless Matt Hancock figure who has to cancel appointments cos the job's too much for him.

SUPERINTENDENT. Well… what about your inquiry?

MANIAC. I've been given eight months and two hundred thousand pounds to come to a verdict. It can wait. The press, however, cannot.

SUPERINTENDENT (*into the phone*). Okay, send her up. The constable will meet her at the lift.

He replaces the receiver.

JOSEPH. Oh right, yup.

JOSEPH *stands and exits*.

SUPERINTENDENT. You can wait next door, m'lud.

MANIAC. No, no, I wouldn't dream of abandoning you now, Andy. We shall face the press together. Brothers in arms. Sultans of swing.

SUPERINTENDENT. But… if she finds out we've got a judge in here, m'lud, she'll stick it in her paper and say the inquiry's been reopened and whatnot and so forth –

MANIAC. Well I won't be a judge then, will I? I'll change character.

SUPERINTENDENT. You'll… what?

MANIAC. It's no problem. I enjoy it. Who shall I be? A maverick crime scene investigator who plays rough but gets results? The ground-down station chief who longs to retire but keeps getting dragged back in? Russell Crowe?

SUPERINTENDENT. Russell Crowe?

MANIAC (*impression*). I can do a pretty convincing Crowe.

DAISY. I don't think you should pretend to be Russell Crowe.

MANIAC. Agreed. Quite hard to explain why he'd be here. What about…?

The MANIAC *looks at the papers, adopting a different voice.*

Forensic Pathologist Captain Mark Poppins who works up in Derby.

DAISY. But there really is a Mark Poppins –

MANIAC. I know, he's in the statement.

DAISY. So… that's quite risky, in't it?

MANIAC. Au contraire, honeybear. If the journo prints something we don't like, we can call the real Mark Poppins and get him to say he wasn't here and therefore she's made it all up…

SUPERINTENDENT. Yes! Brilliant!

The MANIAC *squats down, facing away from the audience and rummages through his bag, finding a new vocal register.*

MANIAC. *Mi mi mi mi mi…*

Knock at the door.

SUPERINTENDENT. Shit, okay, she's here… Come in!

JOSEPH *opens the door.*

JOSEPH. Fi Phelan, sir.

FI PHELAN *enters with a broad smile, holding her phone. She has a tote bag slung over her shoulder, with a dark loaf of bread and a huge bunch of chrysanthemums poking out.* JOSEPH *follows.*

PHELAN. Hi. Hi, guys. Thanks so much for this.
Superintendent Curry?

He goes in for a handshake.

SUPERINTENDENT. Call me Andy. Lovely to meet you.

PHELAN. Okay sure. Mind if I grab a quick selfie?

SUPERINTENDENT. If you grab a quick what now sorry?

She takes a quick selfie with him on her phone.

Oh right, yes, no that's… no problem. I'm so sorry to keep you waiting, by the way. I hope they looked after you downstairs?

PHELAN. I got a cup of very scummy tea, yeah. And the sweaty guy on reception asked if I was feeling alright –

SUPERINTENDENT. Well that's all part of our new Met inclusion and engagement initiative to build community trust.

PHELAN. Right, yeah. You could also try hiring people who aren't white men. That might help too.

SUPERINTENDENT. Well we're actually quite a diverse place here, aren't we, Constable?

JOSEPH. Uh… are we?

SUPERINTENDENT. Just a bit. I'm left-handed for one thing. And we've got a woman on the floor below. Send her up actually –

PHELAN. It's okay. I believe you.

DAISY. And my wife's from Wales so…

PHELAN looks at him, confused. DAISY points at her bag.

You've just been to the shops.

PHELAN. Oh. No, actually, Peckham farmer's market. I'm addicted to buckwheat chia bread.

SUPERINTENDENT. Oh no.

PHELAN. In a good way.

SUPERINTENDENT. Oh great. This is Detective Daisy by the way. As you can tell from his… deductive prowess.

DAISY. DI Dan Daisy, hey, how's it going, you smell amazing.

PHELAN. Okay that's creepy.

They shake hands. PHELAN yelps a little.

DAISY. Sorry, I've got a very firm grip.

PHELAN. So I see –

SUPERINTENDENT. Firm grip of the facts!

They laugh.

DAISY. Yeah. And I'm into rock climbing.

SUPERINTENDENT. This is Constable uh… it's gone again –

JOSEPH. Joseph. Hi.

PHELAN shakes his hand.

SUPERINTENDENT. And finally, a visiting forensic pathologist, Captain…

The MANIAC turns around. He has on a fake moustache, an eyepatch, a wig and brown leather gloves.

Mark Pop… pop-pop-pop…

MANIAC. Captain Mark Poppins. My handshake's also rather firm, but that's because it's wooden. Little souvenir from Afghanistan.

The MANIAC *sneezes violently, holding his wig in place.*

Yikes! Do excuse me, I'm allergic to pollen. And inherited wealth.

PHELAN. OMG, sorry, I'll back off...

MANIAC. No, no, not your fault per se. Please take a seat, Miss Phelan. And by all means put your bag down.

She sits, and rummages in her bag, leaving it on. The MANIAC *flaps, clearing the air.*

SUPERINTENDENT. Can we offer you a drink? Tea? Coffee? There's prosecco somewhere –

PHELAN. I'd rather get a wiggle on if that's cool. I need to upload the article tonight. I'm going to Soho Farmhouse on the weekend.

SUPERINTENDENT. Oh how nice.

PHELAN. It's absolutely fine. So I have a question for you first, Detective, I hope you don't mind if I record this?

DAISY. Oh uh, is that the question?

PHELAN. And another one after that.

DAISY. Right, cos we'd rather not –

MANIAC. Record away, Miss Phelan!

(*Sotto, to* DAISY.) Golden rule of improv: never block.

PHELAN *sets up her recording.*

DAISY (*hissing at the* MANIAC). But if she tapes it we can't deny anything later on –

PHELAN. Is there a problem, guys?

MANIAC. No, no, not at all. The detective here was just saying what an avid reader he is of your articles.

PHELAN. Oh really? Which ones?

DAISY *looks at the* MANIAC *for some steers.*

MANIAC. Well, your... top-tens, I imagine. That's the main output of the hard-hitting reporter these days, is it not? Top-ten cakes, Adam Driver films, genocides, stop me when I get one, fonts, owls, superfoods –

PHELAN. I've done one on fonts, yeah.

MANIAC. Thought so. And the detective here loved it.

PHELAN. Did he really?

DAISY. I really did yeah. Please do... ask away.

PHELAN. Great. So...

(*Starts the recording.*) Why is it you've been called 'The Window-Straddler'?

DAISY. Oh for...!

PHELAN. Or 'The Straddling Detective'.

MANIAC. Ooh... you're like a rat up a drainpipe, aren't you?

SUPERINTENDENT. Who calls him that?

PHELAN. Several climate-change protesters that were interrogated in this station have been using it –

SUPERINTENDENT. Oh, that lot! That's fine then, I thought you meant by other coppers.

MANIAC. Truth be told, he'll straddle anything, Miss Phelan. He's famous for it. You plonk it in front of him, he'll park himself on like it's a see-saw. He'll straddle you if you stay here too long.

DAISY. I won't. I won't do that. Until we get to know each other and clear consent has been granted.

PHELAN. Uh-huh. Because one of these protestors told me some pretty wild stories about your interrogation technique, Detective.

DAISY. Okay, whatever, like what?

PHELAN (*reads*). 'Detective Daisy made me sit on the fourth-floor windowsill with my legs dangling off the edge, then started insulting me, prodding me, saying things like "Why don't you just jump, you useless piece of shit, everyone wants you dead, what's the matter, too scared, little boy"...'

SUPERINTENDENT. Oh as if!

MANIAC. Pfff... sounds a bit Channel Four to me –

PHELAN. So what? They're all lying are they?

DAISY. I didn't put the Anarchist guy on the windowsill, yeah? I couldn't have got him up there for one thing, he was a pretty stocky bloke. Those kids you're talking about were skinny little streaks of piss –

PHELAN. Oh so you could get them up there?

MANIAC. Had he wanted to. He's strong. So what? That's not a crime. Is it? Is that what you want at your paper? To make it illegal to be strong?

PHELAN. I'm literally just passing on what they said...

MANIAC. Well it's absurd! Suggesting that we stick every suspect out the window and shake 'em about like a dirty doormat! I ask you...!

The SUPERINTENDENT *shakes the* MANIAC's *hand.*

SUPERINTENDENT. Well said, m'lud.

MANIAC. Captain. Careful of the hand.

DAISY. Nice one.

The SUPERINTENDENT *slaps the* MANIAC *on the back. His wig dislodges a bit.*

MANIAC. And watch the wig!

PHELAN. So, assuming you didn't dangle him out of the window, why is there no forensic record of his parabola?

DAISY. His what?

PHELAN. Parabola.

JOSEPH. Maybe he didn't have one.

SUPERINTENDENT. Yes, not everyone has everything.

DAISY. What's a palabola?

SUPERINTENDENT. My cousin Ben hasn't got a belly button –

MANIAC. I'll field this one gentlemen: parabola, from the Italian, *parabola*, meaning the arc with which something falls to the earth.

PHELAN. Isn't in the inquiry, exactly.

SUPERINTENDENT. Well… so?

> PHELAN *heads to the window. The* MANIAC *wheels away from the flowers and wafts the air as she passes.*

PHELAN. So if we knew how he fell, we'd know if he was dead or alive when he left the window. Whether he jumped or was dropped…

SUPERINTENDENT. Right. Well. We don't tend to record parabolas.

DAISY. I wouldn't even know how.

PHELAN. What about phone calls? You record them though, right? Except in this case, when we want to confirm the exact time nine-nine-nine was called, the tapes just disappear…

SUPERINTENDENT. Why would you need those?

PHELAN. Because emergency services say the call for the ambulance came in at two minutes to midnight but witnesses at the scene say the Anarchist landed at exactly three minutes past.

MANIAC. Uh-huh. I'm not hearing a question.

PHELAN. Well doesn't it all seem a bit convenient that this tape has just suddenly vanished?

MANIAC. It does actually. For once something goes our way!

PHELAN. As in… a bit too convenient.

MANIAC. Aha! A cover-up, you mean?

DAISY. Now hang on a minute…

JOSEPH. There definitely isn't a cover-up.

SUPERINTENDENT. You wouldn't know, you're far too junior. But he's right, there isn't –

MANIAC. Well now… that's a bit rich, is it not? For a journalist, a hack, a Fleet Street flesh-eater –

PHELAN. We're now based in Bermondsey actually –

MANIAC. To come in here and start accusing *us* of foul play.

SUPERINTENDENT. Hear hear!

MANIAC. When you consider the abuse of trust and violation of privacy executed by the grubby little goblins of the press in recent years. Goodness me, that's a bit much! After your behaviour. Spying on victims of crime! And, worse still, celebs! All of which, okay, could only have taken place with the underhand assistance of the Metropolitan Police but still!

SUPERINTENDENT. Disgraceful!

MANIAC. After the fake news, the clickbait, the assault on our very democracy! Oh that's rich! That's too rich for me and I like a bhuna. To come here and lecture us! It's an outrage!

SUPERINTENDENT. Well said, that man!

He slaps the MANIAC*'s back again. The wig moves forward/comes off. The* MANIAC *replaces it urgently.*

MANIAC. Careful!

The MANIAC *sneezes. And arranges his wooden hand into a pointing finger and places the finger under his nose.*

PHELAN. I'm sorry you feel that way, Captain –

MANIAC. *I'm* sorry I feel that way. It's giving me a rash, although that might just be the chrysanthemums…

He sneezes again.

SUPERINTENDENT. Get the captain some water, Constable.

JOSEPH. Yes, sir.

JOSEPH exits.

MANIAC. And maybe put the bag down –

PHELAN (*ignoring him*). But even if we forget the 'lost' tape, how was it that an ambulance was called before the Anarchist fell from the window?

MANIAC. We plan ahead! So what? We always need ambulances after interrogations at this place, Miss Phelan, it's common sense to call a few in advance...

SUPERINTENDENT. Brilliant!

DAISY. Or it could be a clocks thing? How do you know what happened first? Our clock might be fast and their's might be slow or vice versa or both –

PHELAN. By five minutes?

MANIAC. Why not? You're not in Switzerland now, love. In this country we have things like tax and the sea and a more creative attitude towards timekeeping. We're free spirits and so are our watches.

PHELAN. And a creative attitude towards interrogation as well, yeah? That would certainly explain the bruises on the back of man's neck, wouldn't it?

DAISY *and the* SUPERINTENDENT *exchange a look.*

SUPERINTENDENT. I have no idea what you mean! And I wasn't even here anyway...

MANIAC. I believe Miss Phelan is referring to rumours about the events of that night that spread from this very building –

SUPERINTENDENT. What rumours?

MANIAC. That just before midnight, the detectives interrogating the Anarchist got frustrated and gave him a spicy old smack on the neck, half-paralysing the guy. He starts wheezing away like a fucked accordion, so the officers present call an ambulance in case he carks it. While they're waiting, they haul him up to the window to give him a bit of fresh air and sort himself out, each thinking the other one's got him, 'You got him?' '*You've* got him?' 'No, you've got him.' 'I've not got him.' And next thing you know, bish bash bosh, we've dropped another Italian.

DAISY *wheels round to the* MANIAC.

PHELAN. Yes, exactly.

SUPERINTENDENT. Don't tell her that! Are you mad?

MANIAC. Yes, famously.

PHELAN. Because you have to admit, guys, that does explain everything. Why the ambulance was called in advance, why there was no parabola, and why the prosecutor came to that pretty batshit conclusion.

JOSEPH *enters with a glass of water and gives it to the* SUPERINTENDENT, *who passes it to the* MANIAC.

MANIAC. What conclusion? Spell it out, sweetcheeks. Stop shilly-shallying.

PHELAN *approaches the* MANIAC *as she speaks.*

PHELAN. That the death of the Anarchist should be considered 'accidental'. Not a 'suicide', as the judicial inquiry later described it, but an 'accident'.

The MANIAC *tries to stifle a sneeze.*

MANIAC. Careful, Miss Phelan –

PHELAN. Which is mega-different, not to mention, mega-suspicious…

The MANIAC *sneezes, throwing the water on the* SUPERINTENDENT.

SUPERINTENDENT. Oh…!

PHELAN. Oh yeah, soz.

PHELAN *backs away. The* MANIAC *passes the empty glass back to* JOSEPH. *And sneezes again, into his hanky.*

MANIAC. Thank you, Constable.

JOSEPH. I'll get some more.

SUPERINTENDENT. What the bloody hell are you doing, man?!

DAISY. Captain.

SUPERINTENDENT. I'm soaked – !

The MANIAC *pats the* SUPERINTENDENT*'s face with his hanky.*

JOSEPH. It was an accident.

DAISY. Maybe put your bag down –

PHELAN (*ignoring him*). Yeah, of course! A lot of accidents seem to happen in here, don't they?

MANIAC. It was not an accident!

PHELAN. Which one?

MANIAC. Neither! Neither the spilt water nor the spilt Anarchist. Everything happens for a reason. We do not believe in accidents here. Nor do we listen to rumours. I, for one, cannot stand Fleetwood Mac. This prosecutor is clearly a cretin or a communist. We believe in facts, we believe in reason, we maintain that the entire concept of the accidental is invalid and must be struck from the record.

SUPERINTENDENT. Yes, exactly!

PHELAN. Oh sure. The prosecutor's verdict is invalid. Just like the alibi from the builders who were with the Anarchist at the time of the bombing was also 'invalid', according to the Judge –

MANIAC. But of course that's invalid. The builders themselves are practically invalids! Do you have any idea what a life of manual labour does to the mind? The paint fumes in the lungs, the cement in the sarnies, talk radio! No, no, the working-class brain is a gloopy gruel of caprice and chaos. Nothing is certain with builders, I assure you, everything they say is an estimate.

SUPERINTENDENT. Ha! Bang on!

JOSEPH *enters with another glass of water. The* SUPERINTENDENT *pats the* MANIAC *on the back forcefully. The wig flies into the* MANIAC*'s hands.*

PHELAN (*approaching the* MANIAC). Of course, so it's a class issue? Quelle surprise…

The MANIAC *sneezes into his wig and puts it back on.*

MANIAC. Please, madam… the flowers!

PHELAN. OMG I'm so sorry –

> PHELAN *jinks back, almost bumping into* JOSEPH, *who narrowly avoids dropping the water.*

JOSEPH. Oop! Careful.

> PHELAN *takes the water off* JOSEPH *and passes it to the* MANIAC.

MANIAC. Thank you.

> As PHELAN *spins back round, the flowers go near the* MANIAC's *nose again. He sneezes. And then throws the water onto the* SUPERINTENDENT, *a little too late to be an accident.*

SUPERINTENDENT. Ahh!

> *The* MANIAC *gives the glass to* PHELAN *who gives it to* JOSEPH.

MANIAC. The water's not working, Constable, get me some brandy.

JOSEPH. Right, where do I…?

MANIAC. Brandy! Quick-sticks!

> JOSEPH *looks around, confused, and exits.*

SUPERINTENDENT. Hells bloody bells, I'm sopping!

DAISY. I'll open the window, sir, try and waft out the pollen particles.

> DAISY *opens the window.*

MANIAC. JUST PUT THE BAG DOWN!

PHELAN. I'll put the bag down.

> PHELAN *takes off her bag and puts it by the wall.*

MANIAC. Apologies, Superintendent. It was the sneeze.

SUPERINTENDENT. 'Sneeze' my complete balls! Frankly. You did that on purpose!

The SUPERINTENDENT *kicks the* MANIAC *in the shin and shrieks in pain, grabbing his foot. The* MANIAC *is totally unmoved.*

MANIAC. Careful of the leg, it's metal.

He pulls up his trouser leg to reveal a large iron boot.

SUPERINTENDENT. What the hell is that?

MANIAC. It's a prosthetic. Lost the real one in Iran for stealing. Horrible business.

PHELAN. No way, really? I thought they cut off fingers for stealing?

MANIAC. I stole some shoes. If you plan to kick me again, Superintendent, may I suggest you target the other leg?

The SUPERINTENDENT *is taking deep breaths to manage his pain. The* MANIAC *starts patting him down with his wig.*

The door opens. It's BURTON. *He wears an eyepatch like the* MANIAC's *and holds a metal box.*

BURTON. Have you got a second, sir?

DAISY. Not for you, no –

SUPERINTENDENT. Yes, fine…

    (*To the* MANIAC.) Stop that!

    (*To* BURTON.) Come in, Burton.

The MANIAC *wrings out the wig and puts it back on.*

BURTON. I won't disturb you, I'm just dropping this off.

SUPERINTENDENT. Right, yeah, what is it?

BURTON. It's a copy of the bomb that went off at the bank.

PHELAN. Oh sick! Not a working one though?

BURTON. Don't worry, miss, it can't go off, there's no fuse in it.

SUPERINTENDENT. Well, uh… put it on the desk, Burton. And in fact, while you're here, shake hands with Daisy.

DAISY. What? No.

SUPERINTENDENT. I don't want beef in the building! Make up at once, that's an order.

DAISY. Alright, alright.

BURTON. He could at least explain why he punched me in the face…

The SUPERINTENDENT *plays this down in front of* PHELAN.

SUPERINTENDENT. It was probably just a joke –

DAISY. Because of the 'running me over and shitting on my body' thing –

BURTON. The what?

PHELAN. Oh wow…

PHELAN *makes a note of this*.

DAISY. In the mime. You were miming it.

BURTON. No I wasn't!

SUPERINTENDENT. Please! We've got visitors –

BURTON. I was minding my own business and this lairy prick comes in and lands one on my eye and pisses off again.

MANIAC. He could have least have done the other eye as well to even it out…

BURTON. Yeah, exactly. What? Who are you? You look familiar…

MANIAC. Maybe because we're both wearing eyepatches.

The SUPERINTENDENT *laughs*.

SUPERINTENDENT. You don't know him…

MANIAC. Captain Mark Poppins, Forensics.

BURTON. Poppins? What? You're not Poppins, I know Poppins, he's based up in Derby.

MANIAC. That's right, I just popped in. Poppins by name, pop-ins by nature.

BURTON. He's not Poppins.

The SUPERINTENDENT *kicks him on the shin.* BURTON *yelps.*

SUPERINTENDENT. Oh yes he is.

BURTON. Oh no he isn't.

DAISY *kicks him from the other side.* BURTON *yelps.*

DAISY. Oh yes he is.

MANIAC. Gentlemen, how many times, this is not a panto!

The MANIAC *takes some sweets from his pockets and throws them into the audience.*

BURTON (*to* DAISY). Don't you start, you thug. I know Poppins, I trained with him.

The MANIAC *kicks him hard in the shin.* BURTON *yelps.*

MANIAC. Leave it.

BURTON. Stop kicking me!

BURTON *kicks the* MANIAC *in the leg and then screams.*

MANIAC. Careful, it's metal.

SUPERINTENDENT. Chill it down! All of you...

BURTON. You bloody bastard – !

SUPERINTENDENT. This lady is a journalist!

BURTON *freezes.*

BURTON. Oh right, shit, sorry, hi.

SUPERINTENDENT. Allow me to... Inspector Burton, this is Miss... uh... Touchie?

PHELAN. Phelan.

SUPERINTENDENT. That's it. Miss Phelan is in the middle of a certain *interview*. About a certain... *incident*. That happened here as in there...

He looks at the window and makes a whistling splat noise.

BURTON. Ah, right. I see.

SUPERINTENDENT. If you'd like to ask Burton anything, Miss Phelan, he is our resident explosives expert.

PHELAN. Hunny P, yeah. So that's a copy of the bomb that went off at the bank, is it?

BURTON. Approximation, really. Given that the original was lost.

PHELAN. But another bomb was recovered though, right? At a shopping mall. Unexploded.

BURTON. Uh… yeah, why do you ask?

PHELAN. Because instead of defusing it and giving it to forensics for testing, as would normally happen, that bomb was immediately taken away, buried and blown up.

BURTON. It… So?

PHELAN. So… why? Once a bomb has exploded any chance of working out where and when it was made is like… really hard.

MANIAC. I'll field this one fellas.

He walks over to the bomb and slides it out of the case.

DAISY. Whoa! Careful – !

MANIAC. I know what I'm doing, Detective, I am a captain after all –

BURTON. Those are real explosives in there –

MANIAC. Relax, Bertie. I've defused more bombs than you've had heart murmurs. I suggest you take this as a free masterclass.

PHELAN. You've defused bombs?

MANIAC. Of course.

PHELAN. With a wooden hand?

MANIAC. A steady hand is essential in the bomb-disposal game, Miss Phelan. The best bomb-defuser I ever met actually had two wooden hands. Took him a while but my

God he was steady. A bomb of this ilk is an absolute
minefield. Literally. It's packed to the gills with timers,
springs, flaps, traps and tricks that the very act of hunting for
a fuse and trying to disarm it could set it off. Convinced?

PHELAN. Yeah, alright, you've convinced me.

MANIAC. I think I've convinced me too.

DAISY. And me and all. Good work, Captain.

He grabs the MANIAC's *hand warmly and shakes it. As*
DAISY *turns away, the wooden hand comes with him.*

MANIAC. Ah, shit, now you've disarmed me! I told you it was
wooden.

DAISY. Oh God, sorry –

He passes the hand back to the MANIAC, *who screws it*
back on.

SUPERINTENDENT. Anything to add, Burton? To show Miss
Phelan here that we're… hard at it.

BURTON. Oh, er, yes, sir, if you look, here are some photos of
the original that we had blown up.

PHELAN. The bomb or the photos?

BURTON *passes her some very large photos.*

BURTON. Yes, exactly. So you can see that this copy's way
more simple than the real one. Whoever made that really
knew what they were doing – old-school pros.

The SUPERINTENDENT *snatches the photos off her.*

SUPERINTENDENT. Well don't show her those –

PHELAN. Military, you think?

DAISY. No! No way –   BURTON. Could be, yeah…

The SUPERINTENDENT *kicks* BURTON *again.*

BURTON. Ahh! What now?

PHELAN. So, hang on, although you knew that a bomb of this
complexity required a professional if not military

background, you nevertheless round up a bunch of climate-change activists and trade unionists, and finally haul in some rando Italian train driver...

MANIAC. Of course the bomb looked complex to *him*, Miss Phelan, but that's hardly a surprise. Look at him. Burton's as thick as a pug. We don't let him use scissors.

BURTON. You what? Who the hell do you think you are? In fact, who are you?

The SUPERINTENDENT *and* DAISY *kick him again.*

SUPERINTENDENT. Shut it, you bloody oaf...

MANIAC. And yeah, sure, these seemingly ragtag protest outfits you mention may *look* harmless.

PHELAN. But... they're not?

MANIAC. No. These people are mad! And a serious threat to our way of life, and the safety of your average hard-working, law-abiding statue. These commie cowards are organised and dangerous and our opposition, our seemingly disproportionately savage opposition, is essential.

SUPERINTENDENT. Hence why we've got undercover agents inside all these groups.

MANIAC. Hence why we look at everyone's texts, emails and online search history.

DAISY. Oh shit, do we...?

SUPERINTENDENT. The public's, not ours.

DAISY. Okay, sweet.

MANIAC. Hence why we have one CCTV camera for every eleven people in this country, and arrest you for booing the Royal Family.

PHELAN. Whoa, sorry, back up a sec... you have agents among trade unions and environmentalists?

SUPERINTENDENT. Oh, well –

MANIAC. Do we ever! And what agents! Absolute heroes, every man jack of them! So devoted to their work are they that some of these brave officers began sexual relationships while undercover and even fathered children! I mean talk about committing to a role. Daniel Day-Lewis wouldn't go that method. And don't you worry, they're not alone. We've got guys everywhere. There'll be some in tonight I expect, in this very theatre.

(*To the audience.*) Any undercover agents in?

Hands pops up from the audience.

VOICES. Sir! / Here, sir! / Over here!

MANIAC. There you go, look.

(*To the audience.*) For future ref, you should always answer 'no' to that question.

VOICES. Sorry. / Will do. / Cheers, yeah.

SUPERINTENDENT. A network of spies is absolutely essential these days, you see...

DAISY. It's how we know what all the activist muppets are up to.

MANIAC. And how we plant weapons and bombs on them in case we want a pretext to arrest them all.

SUPERINTENDENT. It – What?

Beat. They all look at him aghast.

MANIAC. To pre-empt Miss Phelan's next remark.

PHELAN. Well it's the obvious conclusion, isn't it? It's hardly likely that some protesters could make a military-grade bomb...

SUPERINTENDENT. Well now *you're* being prejudiced.

PHELAN. What? No I'm not, I loathe prejudice –

SUPERINTENDENT. Suggesting that just because these people are young and poor they can't make anything of themselves. That's elitist.

PHELAN. I... No, come on...

MANIAC. Haha! Love it, Andy. The old switcheroo.

SUPERINTENDENT. Thanks, Captain.

He shakes the MANIAC's *wooden hand. Again it comes off.*

Oh shit, your hand...

MANIAC. Keep it, I've got a spare. I'll do a little switcheroo of my own.

The MANIAC *takes out a hook from his bag and screws it on.*

PHELAN. So, for the record then: this is a deliberate police tactic?

SUPERINTENDENT. Uh... What's that sorry?

PHELAN. Making all protest movements look more dangerous than they really are?

MANIAC. But of course it is!

DAISY. A hook? Have you gone fucking nuts?

MANIAC. Sixteen times actually.

BURTON. I've definitely seen him before...

PHELAN. Because it's super-troubling to hear a policeman actually admit to this...

MANIAC. Troubling? Surely it's reassuring! When this ship goes down, these rozzas are the ones making sure you first-class passengers get all the lifeboats. For it is not free markets, it's not Adam Smith's 'invisible hand' that is safeguarding your way of life, it's the very visible hand of the furious copper, hurtling towards the face of anyone who fancies something different.

PHELAN. Well hang on, it's not *my* way of life. I went to the climate protest, the Black Lives Matter rally, the cost-of-living march.

MANIAC. The lady doth protest too much methinks.

PHELAN. It's not me, alright? I drive an electric car. And I vote Labour.

The MANIAC *starts laughing wildly.*

MANIAC. It's all of us! You, me, them, everyone in here!
I know we all talk a good game. I know we're all nice, right-on, reconstructed liberals who jeer at all the backward bigots out there, but that's only because it doesn't cost us anything. It doesn't matter what we say. Or think. That's just theatre. It's not real, look.

The MANIAC *puts his head through a wall.*

This is about where we live, what we have, where our kids go to school. Our effects, not our causes. Because that's how the police work out who they're working for. The more you've got in the bank, the more we've got your back!

SUPERINTENDENT. That's not our official policy, by the way. Captain Poppins can be a bit eccentric.

BURTON *grabs the* SUPERINTENDENT.

BURTON. That's it! That's how I know him! He's that bonkers bloke from earlier!

MANIAC. Some people think I'm bonkers, but I just think I'm free.

BURTON *rushes over to the* MANIAC.

BURTON. Look!

He pulls off the MANIAC's *eyepatch.*

You see? He's a fake. He's got a real eye under there!

The MANIAC *pulls away* BURTON's *eyepatch.*

MANIAC. So have you, what's your point?

The MANIAC *lets go and the eyepatch pings back into* BURTON's *black eye.* BURTON *yells in pain.*

PHELAN. So okay: are you prepared to admit that the bomb was planted among a group of protesters to give you an excuse to arrest them?

MANIAC. Sure, why not? We do it all the time.

PHELAN. OMG, this is huge... this is Pulitzer huge...

BURTON *starts to remove the* MANIAC's *metal foot.*

BURTON. You see? He's got a real foot as well!

DAISY. We know –   SUPERINTENDENT. Stop!
                                     Get off him –

PHELAN. And so what if he's got a real eye and real foot? It
  doesn't change anything he's saying –

BURTON. It does! He's a fake! An actor! He's just some
  bullshit artist –

SUPERINTENDENT. Burton!

MANIAC. It's fine, Andy, I don't mind, all great artists were
  unappreciated in their time –

BURTON. He's got this condition: 'hystericalmania' or some
  shit. He's not ex-military or anything…

PHELAN. So who is he?

BURTON. He's a total –

  DAISY *runs over and puts his hand over* BURTON*'s mouth
  and spins him away. The* SUPERINTENDENT *pulls out the
  chair at the desk and they sit* BURTON *down and put the
  telephone receiver to his ear.*

SUPERINTENDENT. 'Scuse us – Inspector Burton has to
  make an urgent phone call.

  The MANIAC *leads* PHELAN *quietly upstage and whispers
  to her. Downstage, the* SUPERINTENDENT *hisses at*
  BURTON.

  Shut the shit up, you thick fuck. If the journalist finds out
  there's another inquiry, we're buggered.

BURTON. There's another inquiry?

DAISY. Yeah that's why… I thought you said you knew who he
  was…

BURTON. Who?

DAISY. Poppins.

BURTON. He's not Poppins.

DAISY. No, we know.

PHELAN. Oh I see! Well that explains everything.

The POLICEMEN *turn round, alarmed.* BURTON *replaces the receiver.*

SUPERINTENDENT. What? No it doesn't! Whatever it was he said, it's not that –

PHELAN. It's all good, Superintendent, I know what's going on here. The 'captain' has told me who he really is.

DAISY. Oh jizz.   SUPERINTENDENT. He…
                               Did he?

PHELAN. He did.

SUPERINTENDENT. But… I hope he made you agree to not print it in your article?

PHELAN. What? No, of course not, I'm going to make him the subject of the whole piece – 'The Undercover Bishop'.

DAISY. The what?

BURTON. Bishop?

The MANIAC *spins round his shirt to create dog collar. They stare at him in shocked silence.*

MANIAC. *Mi mi mi mi mi…* Hello there, my name is the Right Reverend Gregory Goosey: bishop, broadcaster, poet, influencer. You may have heard me on Radio Four's *Thought for the Day.*

BURTON. Are you ff– !

MANIAC. Language, my child. Forgive me for concealing my true identity, but I have been sent to you on a special, secret mission: to observe the Metropolitan Police from within. To bear witness to the sin and calumny that so bedevils this institution with mine own eyes.

PHELAN. Okay, but like why?

MANIAC. When a body is dying, the family send for a priest, do they not? And with this constabulary so incapable of internal repair, it is only natural that they would seek help from an independent moral watchdog. And who better than one with vast, recent experience of becalming reputational storms and becooling legal hot water: the Catholic Church. Glossing over institutional abuse since 380AD.

The MANIAC *takes a wafer out of his pocket and presents it to the* SUPERINTENDENT.

And he took bread, and gave unto them, saying, this is my body which is given for you. Eat me, I'm gluten-free.

SUPERINTENDENT. Oh right, yes.

The SUPERINTENDENT *kneels and eats it. And winces.*

Mm. It's a bit furry…

MANIAC. I've been undercover for three months.

BURTON. No. Sorry. This is too far. I can't take any more of this toss.

DAISY *wheels* BURTON *to the front of stage on the chair.*

DAISY. Look, we know he's full of shit, alright, but he's doing it all to save us, so just… have faith in him.

BURTON. Oh, he's our redeemer, is he? Bloody hell, he moves in mysterious ways.

DAISY *squats down and eats a wafer too.* DAISY *pulls* BURTON *in front the* MANIAC.

DAISY. Just get on your knees and eat a wafer.

BURTON *goes to eat a wafer but the* MANIAC *has switched hands and* BURTON *gets the hook in his mouth.*

MANIAC. Looky here! I've caught a whopper! We're gonna need a bigger boat!

BURTON *shouts something garbled as the* MANIAC *twists the hook out of his mouth.* BURTON *grabs his mouth in pain.*

PHELAN. Is he alright?

MANIAC. His mouth's been pierced by God's grace, is all. His tongue's all holey.

(*To the* SUPERINTENDENT.) Hold him still a sec. A dab of holy water will calm his spirit…

The MANIAC *takes out a holy-water pot with sprinkler and flicks some onto a wailing* BURTON.

SUPERINTENDENT. Are you sure that'll work?

MANIAC. Well see what you think.

He chucks the rest of the pot onto the SUPERINTENDENT.

SUPERINTENDENT. Oh…!

MANIAC. And now that my true nature has been revealed, I can finally offer this police force the most liturgically urgent service of all.

BURTON *clambers to his feet and takes the police crest off the wall and writes on it with a marker pen from the desk.*

SUPERINTENDENT. As in… forgiveness?

MANIAC. Forgiveness, what? We stopped doing that decades ago in this country – do you not go on Twitter? No, no, exorcism!

DAISY. What the f– ?

MANIAC. The power of Christ compels you!

He slaps DAISY. *Then turns to* PHELAN.

For it is with the zeal of a religious crusade that this institution must be purged of its heretical element and its scandals publicised as widely as possible…

SUPERINTENDENT. What?!

BURTON *has written 'he's insain' on the crest and waves it at* DAISY *and the* SUPERINTENDENT.

DAISY *rushes over to him and wrestles it off him.*

MANIAC. And fear not, for as we have seen time and time again, rather than lessen your authority, this will allow you to erect a more solid and secure platform for your power!

DAISY *throws the sign out of the open window before* PHELAN *can see it.*

PHELAN. So, sorry, your holiness, let me get this straight: scandals are... good?

MANIAC. Oh they're fantastic. Scandal is to society what confession is to the sinner. It's a catharsis, you see? A laxative that keeps us regular but fixes nothing: the hostile environments, the sewage in the seas, the peerages for political donors. And what's the result? Do we arrest anyone? Can we change anything? Of course not. There's no need! In glorious democracies like ours we get to moan about it instead. Isn't it awful? Aren't they terrible? Yummy yummy yummy and... blockage released. Now back to the football.

SUPERINTENDENT. Well hang on, things are changing a lot around here. We've got a new Met Commissioner, a new Chief Inspector, a new queen, as in king –

MANIAC. Oh the actors change, of course, but the roles remain the same. I mean why do you think this case feels so eerily familiar? Why do you think an Italian train driver falling out of this window fifty-odd years ago still merits re-examination? Because it keeps bloody happening. Because these incidents are a bit too frequent to be 'accidents'. Because 'a few bad apples' may in fact be a sign of a bad tree. Because behind decades of 'individual' cases, from Stephen Lawrence to Chris Kaba, from spycops to Sarah Everard, there is a police force that cannot or will not reform; that still sings the same old abusers' lament: 'I'm sorry, I love you, I can change... but I don't accept the language of the findings...' A force that to this day still employs, protects and even promotes racists, rapists, killers and bullies, and refuses to even admit that there's a problem until it gets caught.* [see page 95]

BURTON *has pulled out his pistol. He points it at the* MANIAC, *wielding it cack-handedly.*

BURTON. Get 'em up!

MANIAC. Oh how thrilling!

DAISY. 'Get 'em up'? Are you serious?!

SUPERINTENDENT. What are you doing, man?

BURTON. What does it look like? Get 'em where I can see 'em...!

PHELAN. Not me though, surely?

BURTON *opens a drawer and takes out some handcuffs.*

BURTON. All of you! Now handcuff yourselves to the radiator.

MANIAC. Oh nice... very hostagey...

BURTON *passes them to* DAISY. *They begin to do it.*

BURTON. I'm sorry it's come to this, but you weren't listening to me, and in a minute you'll understand why I had no other option.

DAISY. Just put the shooter down, dickhead!

BURTON. No. You. Father Poppins bullshit, tell them who you really are...

SUPERINTENDENT. No, Burton –

BURTON. Now!

MANIAC. Happily. Although it may go down like a shit in a submarine. I suggest I fetch my medical records.

BURTON. Fine.

The MANIAC *rummages in the bag.*

But no more wigs or costumes or whatnot or I will shoot you.

MANIAC. Alright, calm down... you sound like the director.

He retrieves the papers and the framed certificate. BURTON *snatches them off him and gives them to the* SUPERINTENDENT, DAISY *and* PHELAN. *The* MANIAC *goes back to his original voice and slowly removes pieces of costume.*

BURTON. There you go. Seeing is believing.

SUPERINTENDENT. A naval engineer... what?

DAISY. He's been in the nuthouse...

MANIAC. Several nuthouses actually.

PHELAN. Paris, New York, Melbourne...

MANIAC. I know. I only need Wimbledon to get the Grand Slam.

SUPERINTENDENT. He's a maniac?

BURTON. A big one.

MANIAC. In my defence, I did mention it.

(*To the audience*.) They can back me up.

SUPERINTENDENT. What? Who's they? What are you talking about?

BURTON. He's mad! He thinks there's an audience watching everything he does. He's seen too much reality TV or something –

PHELAN. Twelve arrests for fraud, four for arson –

SUPERINTENDENT. Including the Great Fire of London.

DAISY. What? That was him?

PHELAN. I mean, it happened in 1666.

DAISY. So no then.

SUPERINTENDENT. Forger as well. And master of disguise.

MANIAC. Oh, thank you very much. Always nice to meet a fan.

SUPERINTENDENT. I'm going to make sure you hang for this... 'm'lud'.

The MANIAC *laughs at this.*

BURTON. Can't touch him I'm afraid, sir. He's certifiable.

DAISY. And you can't hang people any more technically.

PHELAN. Oh tits! There goes my article then. If he's mad, everything he's said is unprintable –

DAISY. And I'll make his face unprintable when I get out of these cuffs...

SUPERINTENDENT. Jesus H Christ on an effing bike to be honest. Coming in here saying he's a judge like that. He scared the living Bee Gees out of me.

MANIAC. Oh yeah? Found that scary, did you? Well say hello to my little friend.

The MANIAC *reveals that he's holding the copy of the bomb. The* OFFICERS *and* PHELAN *recoil in shock.*

PHELAN. Ah...!

BURTON. What are you doing now? Stop playing silly buggers!

MANIAC. But I am a silly bugger, Inspector. I'm rather afraid that's my role in all this. Now drop the gun before I set this thing off, there's a good chap.

PHELAN. What? No, please, I can't die now, I've got a skiing holiday booked –

SUPERINTENDENT. Don't worry, Miss Phelan, he's bluffing. The bomb's been defused –

DAISY. That's right, he's bluffing!

MANIAC. Well let's see. You're the expert round here, aren't you, Bertie? See if you can spot a fuse in all this?

He holds out the bomb.

What's that there? Peeking out like a pube in the pâté? Looks like a ZX6A Longber Acoustic Fuse to me.

The MANIAC *takes the gun from* BURTON.

I'll have that, Bertie. Put the key on the desk and cuff yourself with the others, there's a love.

BURTON *puts the key on the desk. And backs off to join the others at the radiator, cuffing himself to it.*

BURTON. But... where did you get that from?

MANIAC. Oh you'd be amazed what they sell at Liberty these days. I only went in for a Diptyque candle. I've also got a little body-cam thingy that I've filmed everything with.

The MANIAC *reveals that he's wearing a body-cam.*

SUPERINTENDENT. What are you going to do with that?

MANIAC. Not sure yet. Upload it online, maybe put it on TikTok, a Netflix true-crime series, maybe even a piece of avant-garde theatre.

SUPERINTENDENT. You'll ruin us, you realise? You selfish sod. We've been nothing but accommodating with you, we've been, I reckon, lovely. In a way. We play along with this whole bloody shitshow and this is how you repay us?

MANIAC. It is, yes. Society needs this story scandalised, processed, run through the collective colon. So that the country can unite behind this villainy and declare with one voice: 'We know all too well that we're up to our necks in shit, and it is for this very reason that we walk with our heads held high!'

DAISY. Yeah, look, whatever, just please, disarm the bomb.

MANIAC. No thanks. In fact, I think I'll leave it here so I'm not rudely interrupted while I make my exit.

The MANIAC puts the bomb on the desk and then turns to face them and, slowly, the audience.

Well, it's been real. I've had an absolute blast, as will you all in a min. Thank you so much for having me. Goodbye. Au revoir. Auf Wiedersehen, pets. Arrivederci.

The MANIAC turns back to the bomb. And reaches inside. BURTON reaches over to the light switch.

And now for the showstopper...

SUPERINTENDENT. No, please...

Blackout.

MANIAC. Ah!! No!! The lights!! Help!! Get off me!! Ahhhhhhh!

There's a long, falling scream from the MANIAC, followed by a distant explosion and flash beneath the window.

SUPERINTENDENT. Oh my absolute God, frankly! What happened?

DAISY. Someone turn the lights back on!

BURTON. It was outside... The bomb must have gone out of the window...

The lights are switched back on by JOSEPH, *who stands at the door holding a glass of brandy.* BURTON *and* DAISY *have swapped places and look a little ruffled.*

JOSEPH. Apologies, it took me a while to track down the brandy.

SUPERINTENDENT. Good work, Constable. And get the key for these cuffs...

JOSEPH. Yes, sir.

The SUPERINTENDENT *snatches the brandy off him as he passes on his way to the table and downs it.*

PHELAN. Where is he? Where's he gone?

JOSEPH. There's no key here, sir.

DAISY. That bloody maniac must have taken it with him.

PHELAN. Oh look, I can actually squeeze my hand out of the cuffs... Thank God for reformer Pilates. Did he run out the door or something?

She slips out of her handcuffs.

JOSEPH. I didn't see anyone...

They all look from the door to the open window.

DAISY. Oh no...

BURTON. Don't tell me he jumped out of the window!

PHELAN. What?!

She runs to the window.

DAISY. What's going on down there? Can you see anything?

PHELAN *looks out the window.*

PHELAN. There's a crowd of people... most of them filming on their phones. Oh no! Oh the poor guy, there he is! How did this happen, do you think?

DAISY. Your guess is as good as mine.

SUPERINTENDENT. I wasn't even here.

PHELAN. What? Of course you were, you were chained to the radiator.

SUPERINTENDENT. Alright, fine.

DAISY. Yeah well that proves we weren't involved then, dunnit? If we were all cuffed up over here.

PHELAN. Yeah, no, that's uh… Huh. I should probably rethink what happened with the other jump in that case. But I don't get it… Why would he do something like that?

BURTON (*sudden thought*). He was afraid of the dark! He said blackouts were death for the actor. He must have made for the only light source he could find – as in down there…

SUPERINTENDENT. Of course! Like a moth to a flame.

JOSEPH. Anything for an audience, right?

PHELAN. He's certainly got one now.

SUPERINTENDENT. Mm. Well… I guess that's what they call getting yourself out there…

DAISY. Making a splash…

PHELAN. Going out with a bang.

They chuckle quietly. And then become very serious.

SUPERINTENDENT. But it's terrible of course.

DAISY. Of course.

SUPERINTENDENT. Anyone who suffers from a raptus, deserves our sympathy.

The OFFICERS *murmur in agreement.*

PHELAN. A what? A raptus?

SUPERINTENDENT. Just a bit. You saw what happened. He was seized by a darkness-induced raptus and jumped out. There was nothing any of us could have done.

DAISY. Nothing at all.

PHELAN. Yeah. Completely. If it's cool with you guys,
I should probably go and like write this up? My editor'll be
pumped. That was I here I mean.

SUPERINTENDENT. Of course. Don't let us keep you.

She gathers her bag and heads to the door.

DAISY. A raptus!

PHELAN (*as in 'goodbye'*). A raptus.

(*Realises.*) What?

SUPERINTENDENT. A raptus did it. Not us.

PHELAN. Oh. Right, yeah, gotcha.

*She leaves, closing the door behind her. The four men left
onstage look at each other. Beat.*

In sync, the POLICEMEN *each take a key out of their
pockets and unlock their cuffs. Beat.*

BURTON. She'd get it.

SUPERINTENDENT. Shut up, Burton! Oh my God!

BURTON. What? It's a compliment if anything.

SUPERINTENDENT. This is exactly why we have the Met
inclusion, diversity and engagement action plan! Do not say
sexist things at work... unless you're absolutely sure no
women are listening.

DAISY. You're alright, I think she's gone.

DAISY *walks back to the door. There is a knock. They all
look at the door.*

SUPERINTENDENT. Come in!

The actor playing the MANIAC *enters as* JUDGE
RANDALL. *He has a thick, black moustache, a large false
stomach, a leather briefcase and a walking stick.*

RANDALL. Good evening. Forgive me for coming so late. Is this the superintendent's office?

BURTON. Not again!

DAISY. Are you winding me up?

SUPERINTENDENT. How are you not dead?

RANDALL. I beg your pardon?

BURTON. Don't play dumb, dickhead. Don't think we can't see through a fake moustache and a fat suit.

DAISY. Right, now the reporter's gone, I'm gonna batter you like a bloody haddock.

DAISY *goes for him.* RANDALL *shields himself.*

RANDALL. What the hell are you doing?

DAISY *hits him.* RANDALL *doubles over wheezing.*

DAISY. Okay, the gut's real...

JOSEPH *inspects his wig.* RANDALL *straightens up.*

JOSEPH. So's the hair.

SUPERINTENDENT. Right. Shit.

RANDALL. What is wrong with you people?

SUPERINTENDENT. Please excuse my colleagues, we thought you were someone else. You look very familiar, you see...

RANDALL. This is how you receive judges, is it?

DAISY. Judges, what?

BURTON. Oh no...

RANDALL. The name's Randall. Judge Arnold Nathaniel Randall.

SUPERINTENDENT. Ah. Right.

RANDALL. Here to conduct a new inquiry into the recent death of an Anarchist that took place in this very room.

I'd like to get straight down to it, if you don't mind, re-examine all the pertinent evidence in painstaking detail. So...

RANDALL *turns to the audience and smiles conspiratorially...*

...let's go back to the beginning, shall we?

Blackout.

The End.

* *In the 2023 Lyric Hammersmith production, the speech on page 86 was as below. If the data is still relevant or can be updated simply, please feel free to use this as an alternative.*

MANIAC. Oh the actors change, of course, but the roles remain the same. I mean why do you think this case feels so eerily familiar? Why do you think an Italian train driver falling out of this window fifty-odd years ago still merits re-examination? Because it keeps bloody happening. Because these incidents are a bit too frequent to be 'accidents'. Because 'a few bad apples' may in fact be a sign of a bad tree. Because behind decades of 'individual' cases, from Stephen Lawrence to Chris Kaba, from spycops to Sarah Everard, there is a police force that cannot or will not reform; that employs, protects and even promotes racists, rapists, killers and bullies; that in the last ten years, of the eighteen hundred officers facing multiple misconduct charges, has fired just thirteen; and refuses to even admit that there's a problem until it gets caught.

www.nickhernbooks.co.uk

facebook.com/nickhernbooks

twitter.com/nickhernbooks